GRAVE DISTURBANCES

Other Books by Geoffrey Abbott

Ghosts of the Tower of London
Great Escapes from the Tower of London
Beefeaters of the Tower of London
Tortures of the Tower of London
The Tower of London As It Was
Lords of the Scaffold
Rack, Rope and Red-Hot Pincers
The Book of Execution
Family of Death
Severed Heads
Mysteries of the Tower of London
Regalia, Robbers and Royal Corpses
The Executioner Always Chops Twice
Lipstick on the Noose – 100 Executed Women
A Beefeater's Grisly Guide to the Tower of London
William Calcraft – Executioner Extra-Ordinaire!
A Macabre Miscellany – One Thousand Bizarre Facts

Photographic work by Christopher Holmes Photography, Kendal, Cumbria

GRAVE DISTURBANCES

A History of the Body Snatchers

Geoffrey Abbott

Yeoman Warder (retd)
HM Tower of London
Member of the Sovereign's Bodyguard
of the Yeomen of the Guard Extraordinary

Eric Dobby Publishing

First published in Great Britain 2006 by
Eric Dobby Publishing Ltd
12 Warnford Road
Orpington, Kent BR6 6LW

ISBN 1-85882 060 X

Printed in India

CONTENTS

ILLUSTRATIONS

Dedicated to all those whose rest beneath the turf was so cruelly disturbed but by doing so, contributed to the progress of medical science without which, so many of us would not be alive today

ACKNOWLEDGEMENTS

Profuse thanks are tendered to all those librarians, curators, curates and clerics who assisted me in digging down inter their records and taking my pick of facts hitherto shrouded by the mists of time.

INTRODUCTION

Few human beings nowadays give much thought to what may physically happen to their bodies after they have died; they take it for granted that their corpses will be sacrosanct, allowed to disintegrate slowly and with dignity in the confines of their coffins, never to be seen or touched again. However, this was not always the case; the possibility that their bodies could be removed and defiled, for whatever reason, occupied the minds of people even as far back as the seventeenth century, as evidenced by the epitaph on William Shakespeare's tombstone in Holy Trinity Church, Stratford; 'Good friend, for Jesus' sake, forbear, To dig the dust inclosed here; Blest be the man that spares these stones, And curst be he that moves my bones'.

The very suggestion that after interment the coffin might once more be exposed to the air, crowbars wrench the lid open, their lifeless cadaver then desecrated, was enough to fill anyone with complete and utter abhorrence. Yet for many decades immediately prior to 1832 that is exactly what took place up and down the country. Within hours of the burial, graves were ruthlessly opened up, bodies brutally pulled out, then sold to those who would later proceed to dismember them – literally cut them into pieces – in the name of medical science. And such were the rewards received in payment from surgeons and anatomists in desperate need of specimens to dissect for the instruction of their medical students, coupled with the inadequacy of crime prevention, that a new type of criminal was bred whose callousness and lack of respect for the dead were beyond belief – veritable jackals in human form.

Who were these men – and their female confederates? What methods did they employ, not only to extract the bodies but also to avoid detection by leaving the grave apparently undisturbed?

How did they bypass the many and varied devices employed by members of the community to thwart them? What deals were struck between them and their 'customers'? And what penalties did they pay, when finally apprehended?

Even more shocking were the identities of those who purchased the cadavers; surely they, as honourable and highly respected members of society, would not connive at such appalling acts of desecration? Nevertheless they not only bought the human remains; some of them, doctors, surgeons, anatomists, articulators, went even further and encouraged their medical students to exhume bodies, even actually taking part in such nefarious deeds themselves, albeit with the highest of motives, for it could be argued that had not such specimens been made available for their 'hands on' instruction, generations of potentially skilled surgeons could have been lost forever and, who knows, perhaps some of us alive today might not even have been born were it not for the expertise of those surgeons who performed life–saving operations on our forebears, surgeons whose only source of anatomical experience had been obtained from the mouldering corpses supplied by the body-snatchers.

Many hundreds, perhaps thousands of graves were thus robbed before the government of the day introduced the necessary legislation, the *Anatomy Act* of 1832, which heralded the end of the gruesome trading in human bodies. Indeed the reader may well come to the conclusion that the well-worn phrase 'Rest in Peace' was a hope as hollow as many of the coffins ultimately became, the 'remains' which literally didn't. And although nowadays it is all a matter of legally encouraged donor cards and organ transplants by consent, one wonders just how many ancient graves across the country lie empty beneath the sod, their erstwhile occupants long since removed by the body–snatchers.

CHAPTER ONE

THE EARLY DAYS

'The time chosen in the dark winter nights was, for the town churchyards, from six to eight o'clock; at which latter hour the churchyard watch was set and the city police also commenced their night rounds. A hole was dug down to the coffin only where the head lay, a canvas sheet being stretched around to receive the earth and to prevent any of it spoiling the smooth uniformity of the grass. The digging was done with short, flat, dagger–shaped implements of wood, to avoid the clicking of iron striking stone.

On reaching the coffin, two broad iron hooks under the lid, pulled forcibly upwards with a rope, broke off a sufficient portion of the lid to allow the body to be dragged out, sacking being heaped over the whole to deaden the sound of the cracking wood. The body was stripped of its grave clothes, which were scrupulously buried again; it was secured in a sack, and the surface of the ground was carefully restored to its original condition – which was not difficult, as the sod over a fresh–filled grave must always present signs of recent disturbance. The whole process could be completed in an hour, even though the grave might be six feet deep, because the soil was loose, and the digging was done impetuously by frequent relays of active men. Transference over the churchyard wall was easy on a dark evening; and once in the street, the carrier of the sack drew no attention at so early an hour. In country churchyards, the work was undertaken at a later hour when the neighbourhood was asleep.'

So recounted Sir Robert Christison, Professor of Materia Medica at Edinburgh University, in his *Autobiography*, published in 1885. Such detailed knowledge was evidence of his rumoured personal participation in the illegal procuring of corpses. But what drove such an eminent personage – he was physician to Queen Victoria – and other similarly learned men to contemplate involvement in such a hideous practice and thereby align themselves with the dregs of the underworld – people who stole bodies purely for financial gain? How could such an appalling state of affairs ever have come about? To appreciate their position, we must first understand the historic background.

Early in the nineteenth century there was a tremendous impetus in the development of surgery, and the future held great promise for those who had ambitions to become surgeons; accordingly many surgical schools sprang up in the major cities, attracting thousands of students. Even in those early years there were nearly a thousand students in London and about the same number in Edinburgh; three hundred in Glasgow, eighty or so in Manchester; forty each in Liverpool and Birmingham, with rather fewer in Bristol and Exeter. But before they could be let loose in the operating theatre they had to be taught the fundamentals of anatomy by their surgeon tutors. Basically they had to know exactly what they would find on cutting open a patient's stomach; they had to be shown the position and function of the various organs and how to diagnose diseased body parts and perform vital operations on them. The method of amputating limbs had also to be demonstrated. In fact everything necessary for them to follow their desired profession required hands-on experience.

Moreover the Corporation of Surgeons required each student to produce a certificate of having attended at least two courses of dissection in order to qualify, and so the surgeons in charge needed many specimens, dead bodies to dissect, to give their students the necessary hands-on experience. The only alternative for students was to qualify via another organisation, the Apothecaries' Hall, which did not demand a certificate, but this of course meant that, having been unable to learn by studying the dead, they could only do so by practising on the living, a high-risk situation for them and even more so for their patients.

At one time there had been no shortages of bodies for, as reported in the *Monthly Chronicle* of March 1888, 'during the long French war, professors, schools and students of anatomy had as plentiful a supply of subjects as they could well desire from the bloody continental battlefields'. But with peace declared that source had dried up, and the only cadavers then legally available were those of the meagre and totally inadequate number of criminals who had been hanged on the city's gallows. This provision was authorised by various *Felon Dissection Acts* which sought to provide a deterrent as additional to being hanged. One as early as 1540 empowered the newly incorporated company known as 'The Maisters or Governours of the Mystery and Comminalte of Barbours and Surgeons of London' to have the corpses of hanged malefactors handed over to them for dissection, it being stipulated that 'the sayd maysters or governours of London & their successours yerely for ever after their said discrecions at there free liberte and pleasure may take without contradiction foure persons condempned adjudged and put to deathe for feloni by the due order of the Kynges lawe of thys realme for anatomies with out any further sute or labour to be made to the kynges highnes his heyres or successors for the same. And to make incision of the same deade bodies or otherwyse to order the same after their said discrecions at their pleasure for their further and better knowlage instruction in sight learnyng & experience in the said syence of facultie of Surgery'.

Similar acts were passed in 1604, 1726 and 1752. In the latter year 'An Enquiry into the Causes of Frequent Executions at Tyburn' contained a statement on page 27 by a Dr Mandeville proposing that bodies of hanged felons be handed over to surgeons. For, as he said, 'Where then shall we find a readier supply? And what degree of People are fitter (more suitable) for it than those I have named? When Persons of no Possessions of their own, that have slipp'd no Opportunity of wronging whomever they could, die without Restitution, indebtd to the Publick, ought not the injur'd Publick to have a title to, and the Disposal of what the others have left?'

And that is exactly what the Act achieved, increasing the availability of corpses by enacting 'That the body of every person convicted of murder shall, if such conviction and execution shall be in the county of Middlesex or within the City of London, or the liberties thereof, be immediately conveyed by the sheriff or sheriffs, his or their deputy or deputies, and his or other officer or officers, to the hall of the Surgeons' Company or such other place as the said company shall appoint for this purpose, and be delivered to such person as the said company shall depute or appoint, who shall give to the sheriff or sheriffs, his or their deputy or deputies, a receipt for the same; and the body so delivered to the said company of surgeons, shall be dissected or anatomised by the said surgeons, or such persons as they shall appoint for that purpose; and that in no case the body shall be suffered to be buried unless after such body shall have been dissected or anatomised'.

This was put into immediate effect. Thomas Wilford, a one-armed lad of seventeen, married his prostitute wife on a Wednesday and murdered her by cutting her throat on the following Sunday. He pleaded innocence on the grounds of jealousy but was found guilty, the judge pronouncing 'Thomas Wilford, you stand convicted of the horrid and unnatural crime of murdering Sarah, your wife. This Court doth adjudge that you be taken back to the place from whence you came; and there to be fed on bread and water till Wednesday next, when you are to be taken to the common place of execution, and there hanged by the neck until you are dead; after which your body is to be publicly dissected and anatomised, agreeably to an act of Parliament in that case made and provided; and may God Almighty have mercy on your soul!'

At that time, and for many years to come, hanging was little more than a slow suffocation, and not surprisingly most criminals recoiled in horror not only at the prospect of their bodies being cut up and anatomised, but that it might even take place while they were still alive! One man who was determined to stop at nothing rather than have his body handed over to the surgeons was William Smith, hanged at Tyburn on 3 October 1750 for forgery. From his condemned cell he had distributed not only an ode on his melancholy condition, but also an advertisement 'entreating contributions for his decent interment and that his poor body might not fall unto the surgeons and thereby perpetuate the disgrace of his family'. The advertisement ended with the plea: 'Those who compassionate my deplorable situation are desired to send their humane contributions to Mrs Browning's, next door to the Golden Acorn in Little Wild Street; and that Heaven may reward their charitable disposition is the dying prayer of the lost and unhappy William Smith'.

Such an appeal must have touched the hearts of many charitable persons, or perhaps those of his former confederates who may have thought: 'There but for the grace of God, go

I!', for the number of contributions received by Mrs Browning amounted to a large sum of money. Negotiations with someone in authority must have taken place, for records show that of the twelve felons hanged that day, only one body was delivered to the surgeons, and it was not Smith's. His was handed back to his friends who buried it in a local cemetery. But it is inconceivable that the body-snatching fraternity would have been unaware of the advertisement – and so no doubt his cadaver finished up on the dissecting table anyway, albeit by a different route!

A condemned man who took the diametrically opposite view to that of William Smith was James Brooke who, in a bid to sell his corpse to a surgeon in order to buy some creature comforts while awaiting the hangman, wrote to Salisbury surgeon Edward Goldwyr, as follows:

> Sir – Being informed that you are the only surgeon in this city, or county, that anatomises men, and I being under the unhappy circumstance, and in a very mean condition, would gladly live as long as I can, but by all appearances I am to be executed next March, having no friends on earth that will speak a word to save my life, nor send me a morsel of bread to keep life and soul together until the fateful day; so if you will vouchsafe to come hither, I will gladly sell my body – being whole and sound – to be ordered at your discretion; knowing that it will rise at the general resurrection as well as from your house as from the grave. Your answer will highly oblige your's, etc. James Brooke
> 3 October 1736, Fisherton-Anger Gaol.

Of course there was always the outside chance that after being hanged and laid out on the dissecting slab, a felon might just recover at the first, preliminary cut by the scalpel, or even sooner, and be resuscitated! As early as 1587 the historian Stow related in his *Annals* that 'The 20 of Februarie, a strange thing happened to a man hanged for felonie at Saint Thomas Wateringes; being begged by the Chirurgions of London to have made of him an anatomie, after hee was dead to all men's thinking, he was cut down, stripped of his apparell, laide naked in a chest, thrown into a carre, and so brought from the place of execution to the Chirurgeons Hall nere unto Cripelgate; the chest there being opened and the weather extreme cold hee was found to be alive and lived till the three and twentie of Februarie and then died'. Which chest was opened, the container or that part of the man's anatomy, was not made clear, but the risk was obviously dire.

William Duel, hanged 23 November 1740 on a charge of rape, also recovered and lived rather longer than the aforementioned; as reported in the *London Daily Post and General Advertiser*: 'Duel was brought to Surgeons' Hall, in order for Anatomy, but after he was stripp'd and laid on the Board, and one of the Servants was washing him, he perceived Life in him and found his Breath to come quicker and quicker, on which a Surgeon bled him and took several Ounces of Blood from him, and in about two Hours he came so much to himself as to sit up in a Chair, groan'd very much and seem'd in great Agitation but could not speak'. The Clerk of the Barber's Company reported that 'he did manage to say 'Don't!' whenever anyone touched him though it was thought to be mostly insensible of anything but paine which in a great measure he endured by his most violent screams and was often in strong convulsions in his bowels, which he then expresst by applying his hands to those parts'.

Later, when capable of speech, he said he did not recall being hanged, but that he had dreamed of being in Paradise, where an angel had told him his sins were forgiven. After three or four days he made a complete recovery and appeared at the next sessions at the Old Bailey where, although legally he could have been hanged again, he was sentenced to be transported for life.

To their understandable dismay, not only were the surgeons deprived of a specimen they intended to dissect, they also had to pay the incidental expenses, viz:

Paid to the Beadles their expenses in bringing the body from Tyburn	£2.19.0
Paid the Officers of the two compters (gaols)	£2.2.0
Paid Joseph Wheeler, the Company's Clerk, for his Coach hire and expences in attending the Sheriffs when the Body came to life	£0.10.0
Paid the Chairwoman for her trouble and expenses about the Body.	£0.5.0.

A similar case was reported to have taken place in Germany, albeit with a less happy ending for the criminal involved. While his body was being stretched out ready for dissection before an audience of surgeons, it was seen to be still alive. It was alleged that the lecturer then said: 'I am pretty certain, gentlemen, from the warmth of the subject and the flexibility of the limbs, that by a proper degree of attention and care, the vital heat would return again and life would be restored. But when it is considered what a rascal we should again have among us, that he was hanged for so cruel a murder, and that, should we restore him to life, he would probably kill someone else; I say, gentlemen, all these things considered, it is my opinion that we had better proceed in the dissection.' Whether this harangue stirred their consciences or not, suffice it to say that they all nodded agreement. Whereupon the lecturer plunged his knife into the breast of the culprit and proceeded to start the lesson.

Whether this story was true or merely mythical, the possibilities were so awful that friends of a hanged felon would help speed his demise by invading the scaffold and pulling on his legs. Further scenes of utter chaos occurred once the body had been cut down, opposition to the officers ordered to convey the corpse to the Surgeons' Hall being reinforced not only by those who, by simply touching the cadaver, believed they would be assured of a cure for their various skin complaints, rashes and tumours, but also by the hangman himself, whose traditional perquisite was that of claiming the often gaudy and flamboyant clothes worn by the felon at this, his last public appearance. And even as today, when orderly protest marches are disrupted by those who delight in stirring up trouble just for the sake of it, so further attacks on the officers and their macabre burden often left little more than a mangled corpse clad in tatters for use by the surgeons. On occasions troops had to be called in to restore order, the cost being met by the surgeons' company, who were also responsible for compensating the hangman over the loss of his perks, together with any members of the mob who claimed for injuries received during the melee.

Sometimes the corpse was captured and spirited away by his friends and later given a decent burial, as is evidenced by an entry dated 6 March 1711 in the records ordering William Cave, a Beadle (a minor parish official responsible for maintaining order) 'to make Inquiry who the persons were that carryed away the last body from Tyburne, and that such persons be Indicted for the same'.

Where the proceedings were conducted in a more orderly fashion, the corpse was transported ceremoniously through the streets in a cart, the other passengers being the hangman and

A public dissection

his assistant. Leading the procession was the City Marshal in full uniform. On arrival at the Surgeons' Hall the dead body was stripped and laid out on a table, later being moved to an operating theatre for dissection. Even such well-organised occasions as this failed to meet everyone's approval, however. Mr Macaulay, a London alderman, expressed his misgivings in an entry in his diary for 6 December 1796: 'Francis Dunn and Will. Arnold were yesterday executed for murder and were conveyed to the new Surgeons' Hall in Lincoln Inn Fields. They were conveyed in a cart, their heads supported by tea chests for all the public to see; I think contrary to all decency and the laws of humanity in a country like this. I hope it will not be repeated'.

Members of the public were frequently invited to attend the dissection classes. The *Daily Advertiser* of 15 January 1742 carried the advertisement: 'Notice is hereby given that there being a publick Body at Barbers and Surgeons Hall, the demonstrations of Anatomy and the Operations of Surgery will be at the Hall this evening and tomorrow at six o'clock precisely in the Amphitheatre'. Sometimes private houses were hired for such events. Six guineas was paid for the use of the house in which the corpse of murderer William Long was dissected, and seven guineas for the hire of a stable yard when Maria Theresa Phipoe's body was operated on. Laurence Shirley, Earl Ferrers, imprisoned in the Tower of London on a charge of murder, was

Earl Ferrers in his coffin

tried and found guilty. When the judge added that he was to be hanged '"after which your body will be delivered to Surgeons' Hall to be dissected and anatomised", the Earl exclaimed "God forbid!", hastily correcting it to "God's will be done!"' When the Earl's corpse had been laid out in Surgeons' Hall, 'a large incision was made from the neck to lower breast, and the throat was opened. The lower part of the belly incised and revealed, whereby the bowels were taken away'. It was later exposed to the enormous number of people who had come to see the spectacle of a member of the aristocracy being dissected, and it remained on public view for three days before being removed and buried.

Although the intention of the Act to meet the needs of the surgeons was well-meant, there were only about seventy-seven felons being executed each year during the period 1805 to 1820 and this was completely inadequate to supplying the needs of the surgical schools. Competition between the surgeons was intense as their incomes were dependent upon the number of enrolled students and so, denied the advantages of modern aids such as plastic skeletons and computer models, they had to adopt more unscrupulous measures; if there were insufficient numbers of criminal corpses available, then the corpses of the innocent would have to be acquired.

One plentiful source of supply was Ireland where graves were robbed almost with impunity by anyone whose greed for money outweighed their moral scruples. The graveyards surrounding Dublin, and in particular those containing the last remains of paupers, provided rich pickings, the gruesome harvest being shipped to lonely parts of the Scottish coast and thence to Glasgow, Edinburgh and London. But this supply was infrequent and insufficient and the bodies far from fresh. Desperate for specimens the students, eager to further their medical careers, took the law into their own hands and far and wide across the country, started to raid their local cemeteries, assisted in some cases by their surgeons! And so commenced the era which became known as the 'Resurrection Days'.

One surgeon was Sir Robert Christison, who recounted what was assumed to be his personal participation in the episode quoted at the beginning of this chapter. Another, a demonstrator of anatomy, led his team to a cemetery, only to be attacked by a number of local residents guarding the graves from just such an invasion. Most of the pupils escaped over the wall but the teacher, in attempting to follow them, had his legs seized by the watchers, while his assistants desperately tugged at his arms. Eventually the locals gave up but, as described later 'the see-saw movement to which the teacher had been subjected on the crest of the wall injured him so severely that it is believed he never quite recovered from its effects'.

It was hardly surprising that young, amateurish and doubtless apprehensive students on nefarious raids would sometimes run into trouble, as evidenced by the occasion when two of them visited a graveyard intent on stealing the body of a recently buried man. All went well and, securing the corpse in a bag, they carried it to a nearby inn where they intended to stay for the evening. Asking for a private room wherein to recuperate over a drink, they were shown into one which happened to incorporate a closed box-bed built into the wall. While supping their flagons of ale, they decided to inspect their booty. Removing it from the bag, they laid it out on the floor; as they did so, they heard authoritative voices in the bar room below, inquiring about two suspicious characters who had been seen in the vicinity. Assuming that they were the wanted men, they hastily bundled the body into the box-bed and made their escape via the window.

Meanwhile the lady of the house permitted the watchmen to search the inn and, satisfied by the discovery of the empty glasses and the open window that their birds had flown, they left the premises. Later, the lady retired to bed, in the very room that she had allowed the students to use. As well as having been her bridal chamber many years before, it was where she had nursed her husband during his recent fatal illness and from where he had been carried out to the waiting hearse. Heavy at heart, burdened with her sad memories, listlessly she went across to the bed and opened its doors – only to collapse in a faint as she saw by the light of the flickering candle, the body of her husband stretched out on the coverlet!

On another occasion three students, ill-equipped for their sortie into forbidden territory, drove out in a gig to a cemetery in which they had learned a farmer's wife had been interred. Leaving the vehicle in a secluded lane in charge of one of their number, the other two located the grave and after much exertion, managed to extricate the coffin and remove the body. It was then that they realised they had forgotten to bring a sack, so one of them knelt to allow his companion to place the body on his back, then held it in place with a firm grip on the winding sheet in which the corpse was swathed. Thus encumbered, he proceeded to stagger forward with his unearthly burden while the other went on ahead to ensure the way was clear of watchmen or passers-by.

The laden student, stumbling over the rough earth, his nerves at breaking point at the thought of what he was doing – and carrying – suddenly realised that the corpse was slipping downwards, its toes dragging along the ground behind him; then horror filled him as he felt the dead woman's knees knocking against the backs of his legs! Panicking, he dropped the body and rushed towards his companions, shouting hysterically: 'She's alive! She's alive!' Despite the knowledge that this was impossible, all three, now utterly terror-stricken, fled the scene as fast as they could.

But they were not the only ones to assume that the farmer's wife still breathed. Next morning her husband, on his way to work in the fields, found her body lying in the lane, her grave-clothes dirty and dishevelled. Instinctively assuming that she had been buried alive and somehow had fought her way out of her living tomb, he shouted for help, then attempted to resuscitate her in whatever way he could. And it was only when confronted by the sight of the disturbed grave and the discarded spades that he was eventually convinced of the true state of affairs, leaving him with a profound sense of guilt for not having guarded her in what should have been her last resting place.

Some of those ventures were indeed traumatic – and not only for the students. When the famous Scottish surgeon Robert Liston was but a student, he happened to read a newspaper report about the funeral of a sailor who had drowned. The account was embellished with a poignant description of the grief suffered by the dead mariner's fiancée. Sensing that the deceased would be a likely specimen for him and his colleagues to dissect, and learning that the cemetery concerned was on a lonely part of the Scottish coast not far away, he and his fellow students took a boat trip, and on landing at nightfall, observed a young woman crouched over one of the graves, sobbing piteously. Taking it for granted that such incidents in graveyards were commonplace on any day of the week, they waited until she had moved away, then pounced and, in a short space of time, had the corpse out and into the boat. On pushing the boat off and manning the oars, they happened to take a last look at the cemetery to see the young woman waving her arms in frenzied fashion, screaming hysterically at the top of her voice, at all that remained of her loved one – the gaping grave, the lidless coffin, the torn shroud. The students increased the speed of their departure.

A similar tragic episode – for the mourner – occurred when other Scottish students heard about a woman who had died in childbirth. Visiting the lonely cemetery, also by boat, on a bitterly cold and windy night, within twenty minutes they had extracted the corpse, a tall blonde-haired woman, from the grave and carried her as far as a dyke they would have to cross. Just as they laid the cadaver on the ground preparatory to wading through the water, they suddenly saw the light of a lantern among the tombstones behind them, accompanied by the barking of a dog; hurriedly they dragged the body across the dyke and towards their boat. As they did so, some of her long fair hair snagged on the rocks, tearing away some of her scalp; frantically the students scrambled aboard the craft together with their ghastly cargo, and cast off, realising as they did so that the person with the lantern had stopped where the body had lain. It was later reported that the man with the lantern was the woman's husband – and that he had recognised the tangled locks of hair..!

Of course the youthful body-snatchers did not escape unscathed every time. One trio had obviously failed to carry out a pre-raid recce before visiting Blackfriars Churchyard in Glasgow. Unknown to them, anti-body-snatcher devices such as trap-guns operated by trip-wires had been installed in the cemetery. In the pitch darkness one student promptly encountered one of these and the devastating hail of shot killed him instantly. His comrades, fearful of capture, hauled his limp corpse out of the cemetery, where they leant it against the wall. Then each tied a leg to one of theirs, and, supporting their erstwhile friend by putting their arms around his waist, they wended their way back to their lodging, swaying and singing as if drunk. Once in the house they deposited the youth's body in his room, circulating the news next day that he had committed suicide!

The hazards of grave–robbing were many and varied; those involved could not relax, even when safely away with the body and heading for home. On one such occasion two students thought they'd taken everything into consideration when planning a raid on a cemetery at Mearns, south of Glasgow. Having extracted the desired corpse from its coffin, they removed the shroud and threw it back into the grave, then dressed the cadaver in the spare suit of clothes they'd brought with them, no easy task on a night dark, with their nerves taut and the body limp and very flexible. They then hauled the corpse to the road and hoisted it on to the seat of their gig, took their places each side of 'him', and set off back to town. All went well until the Gorbals tollbar came in sight. As the keeper, an elderly man, resentful at having to come out and collect their toll money at that time of night, approached and looked up at them, for one heart-stopping moment the youths thought the game was up – but, thinking rapidly, one started to tender the required sum while the other allowed the corpse's head to droop on to his shoulder. Putting his arm round the dead man, he soothed the icy brow and made encouragingly sympathetic noises to his 'friend'. The tollman, observing his efforts, looked at the 'sick' passenger, and the two students restrained a deep sigh of relief as the man exclaimed: 'Oh! puir auld bodie, he looks unco ill in the face! Drive cannily hame, lads, drive cannily!' They did!

The students and their instructors were not the only medical men to disinter corpses, of course. For many years a doctor was in the habit, not only of digging up his own deceased patients, but of boasting of the fact to his colleagues in the surgical schools. On one occasion, after having dug up the body of a young man he had lately been attending, he met his ex–patient's mother walking along the road. She was naturally distraught at the rumours being circulated about body-stealing in the area, and the doctor gave her a lift home in his gig and soothed her fears, saying that he had just passed the cemetery and all was well. However he omitted to add that her son's corpse lay beneath the very seat on which she was seated! The same gentleman once commented to a friend that he had actually kept his promise to a woman that he would make sure her body would not fall prey to body snatchers; he stole her body himself!

Not everyone got away with it, however. On 9 March 1742, when a corpse was discovered near the house of an Edinburgh surgeon, Martin Eccles, infuriated crowds seized the Portsburgh Drum (traditionally used to warn the inhabitants of impending attack) and marched through the Cowgate, then proceeded to smash his shop and scatter his possessions in the street. That year was particularly momentous for Edinburgh, body-snatching-wise, for just over a week later the house of a gardener, Peter Richardson, was set on fire by a mob who suspected that he had been involved in exhuming corpses from the local cemetery, and on 26 March a chairmaster (sedan chair) and a carrier were not only banished from the city when the passenger was found to be a cadaver, but their chair was publicly burnt by the executioner. Nor was that the end of body snatching activities that year, for in the following July another gardener, one John Samuel, who had also wielded his spade more profitably than by just digging up swedes or tatties, was whipped through the city streets for having been caught selling the body of a child which had been buried in Pentland Kirkyard a week earlier, and he was then banished from Scotland for seven years.

But during the decades to come, the need for surgical specimens remained desperate. In 1814 Doctor Granville Sharp Pattison and his students heard of recent burials in two local cemeteries, the Cathedral and Ramshorn graveyards in Glasgow, and were determined to procure them for dissection purposes. Two raiding parties set out; the Cathedral raid was highly successful, two corpses being procured, but the Ramshorn students were attacked and pursued by the police, though they escaped with their prey. Search warrants were obtained, the police accompanied by relatives together with a dentist who had lately attended one of the deceased. They visited Dr Pattison's rooms and, in the presence of the doctor and students, searched meticulously but without success. However just as they were about to leave, the dentist recalled seeing a tub of discoloured liquid in one of the rooms. Returning, he plunged his hand to the bottom of the tub, to find not only some fingers and other body parts but a jawbone, the teeth of which he identified to be those of his late, and missing, patient.

Arrested, the accused men were escorted to gaol under a strong guard while the mob vented its fury by shattering the windows of the doctor's house, a fury which was exacerbated by a later discovery of more bodies hidden beneath the floorboards. At the subsequent trial, guarded in the dock by men armed with bayonets, Pattison, his lecturer Andrew

Russell, together with students Robert Munro and John McLean expected the worst, but such was the reluctance of the authorities to take decisive action against such 'crimes' – after all, in the eyes of the law, no-one owned a body – that the question of convincing identification was not resolved and all were released on payment of a fine.

About the same time, Glasgow was also the scene of another horrendous drama, when a consignment consisting of bags labelled cotton or linen rags, arrived at the docks from Ireland, addressed to a salesman of dubious character who lived in Jamaica Street in that city. When faced with freight charges of nearly £60, he refused to accept the cargo and returned it to the dock authorities who promptly stored it away in a warehouse. After some weeks workmen entering the building were almost overcome by the foul stench which greeted them, and to the horror of those unfortunate enough to be detailed to investigate, the putrefying corpses of several men, women and children were discovered in the bags.

Enquiries by the authorities revealed that the consignment had been sent by Irish students, bound (in more ways than one) for the anatomy schools of Edinburgh and Glasgow, but they had failed to notify the huckster in time; upon the shocking news spreading throughout the city no doubt that gentleman kicked himself for failing to inspect the delivery before sending it back, for at a going rate of ten to twenty guineas per cadaver, he would have shown a handsome profit over and above the freight charges demanded!

There were, of course, cases where entire bodies were not needed. One surgeon employed by Bristol Infirmary seized the opportunity to sever the head of a patient who had just died, then despatched the decapitated cadaver in its coffin to the relatives. However the recipients, concerned about recent reports of body snatchers, unscrewed the coffin lid, only to recoil in horror at the sight which confronted them. Incensed, they descended on the hospital, the uproar resulting in one of the doctors appearing at an upper window and asking them what they wanted. 'What do I want?', shouted the man leading the crowd, 'I want my son's head – and if I don't get it, I'll have yours!' At which threat, the head was handed over and the triumphant mob dispersed.

A similar instance arose in America where another medical man, Dr John Francis, who at that time was studying the human brain, took advantage of the death of one of his patients to decapitate the body, assuming that the coffin would not be opened. The dead man was George Frederick Cooke, an English actor born in London in 1756, who had emigrated to America to further his career. However during his elaborate funeral his thespian colleagues were permitted to view the body prior to the burial in St Paul's Cemetery in New York – and the shocking truth was revealed.

When challenged, Dr Francis denied all knowledge of the ghastly mutilation, but on his death he bequeathed the skull to a friend, Dr McClellan, who in turn passed it to Dr Ross Patterson of a Philadelphia medical college. After a century or so it was eventually decided that the skull should be reunited with its torso and so the grave was opened up, the coffin lid raised, and the skull reverently (at last) placed alongside the other bones. However it was reported that sometime during the preceding years Cooke's skull was loaned to the famous actor Edwin Booth, who used it as a stage prop for Yorick's skull ('I knew him well') while taking the lead part in Shakespeare's *Hamlet*!

Another, even more extraordinary instance of just a head being stolen, was reported in the *Scottish Courant* of 13 November 1828. In a case tried before the Middlesex Sessions on the previous Thursday, three men were charged with breaking open a vault in a church in Hendon, in which there were some dead bodies. Selecting one in particular, they then proceeded to sever the head. The reason given to the court was bizarre, to say the least, for one of the accused was a surgeon, and the body he had thus decapitated was that of his mother! He went on to explain that there was an hereditary disease in his family, the causes and nature of which he wanted to investigate in order to prevent himself succumbing to it, and believed that if he could obtain his mother's head and dissect it, he might ascertain vital anatomical evidence. Whether the court believed his story or not, all the prisoners were found guilty and severely punished.

But these and other efforts of the members of the medical profession and their students to acquire specimens did not go unnoticed; it was not long before the criminal classes, the hard men of the underworld who would stop at nothing to make a few guineas, soon began to realise that here was a market that could have been created specifically for their benefit. Their reasoning was simple; why risk confrontation, possible injury and arrest by picking pockets, holding up a stagecoach or burgling a wealthy merchant's house when, all over the country, there existed cemeteries, usually isolated and avoided by the general public, in which, on an almost daily basis, potential sources of income were being buried? And so by the end of the eighteenth century the days of the amateur, the forays of the young, enthusiastic but unskilled students were drawing to a close. The real professionals would now take over!

CHAPTER TWO

ENTER THE BODY SNATCHERS

Body snatching was not new, of course. As early as 1711 the records of the Edinburgh College of Surgeons included entries deploring the violation of sepulchres in Grey Friars Churchyard, and a decade later apprentices in that city had a clause inserted in their indentures warning them not to violate graves. In England cases involving notorious criminals came to the public's attention, not least that of Jonathan Wild. Hanged at Tyburn in 1725, his remains were obtained by relatives and friends and interred in St Pancras' churchyard, appropriately at the dead of night. Jonathan had not escaped the gallows, nor did he escape the body snatchers, for a few days later his coffin was found empty and abandoned in Fig Lane, and the suspicion that the surgeons had received yet another specimen on which to practice was borne out by the fact that his skeleton finished up in a glass case in the museum of the Royal College of Surgeons in London.

Another snatch was that of the body of the famous, or infamous, highwayman, Dick Turpin, who was hanged at York on 10 April 1739. As the *Newgate Calendar* reported: 'The spectators of the execution seemed to be much affected at the fate of this man, who was distinguished by the comeliness of his appearance. The corpse was brought to the Blue Boar in Castle Gate, where it remained till the next morning, when it was interred in the churchyard of St George's parish, with an inscription on the coffin bearing the initials of his name and his age. The grave was made remarkably deep and the people who acted as his mourners took such measures as they thought would secure the body; yet about three o'clock on the following morning some persons were observed in the churchyard, who carried it off; and the populace, having an intimation whither it was conveyed, found it in a garden belonging to one of the surgeons of the city. Hereupon they took the body, laid it on a board, and having carried it through the streets in a kind of triumphal manner, filled the coffin with unslacked lime and buried it in the grave where it had before been buried'.

With the advent of the professional gangs the practice became really widespread. There was, of course, no dearth of targets, all towns and even villages having their own graveyards. Some of the plum pickings were to be had in places such as St Saviours, St Giles, St Pancras and Moorfields in London, the cemeteries of Manchester, Liverpool and Carlisle, in fact any town having extensive graveyards, and of course the small ones in villages as these were more likely to be unprotected. And except for the families whose relatives' bodies had been stolen, public opinion was for the most part remarkably unconcerned, as were members of the Government who, in any case, were intent on keeping the Army well provided with a sufficient number of trained surgeons and so were prepared to overlook such 'social misdemeanours'. Nelson was not the only one capable of turning a blind eye! A careful balance had to be maintained by the authorities; public outrage and consequent riots had to be avoided at all costs, yet the supply of corpses was vital for medical training. Subterfuge was the only answer. For instance when a consignment of cadavers arrived from Dublin, the ship was boarded by the police who proceeded to impound the containers. On witnessing this, the customer, a surgeon who had been eagerly waiting on the quayside for the delivery of his new stock of specimens, wasted no time in complaining to the Home Office. Discreet instructions were instantly forthcoming, resulting in the same conscientious constables loading the barrels on to wagons and no doubt giving them a police escort to their surgical destination!

The qualifications required by a body snatcher (otherwise known as a sack-em-up man, a stiff-lifter or, in rural Warwickshire, a diggum upper) were well-defined. Low cunning and quick wittedness rather than intelligence were essential; he had to be strong, for corpses are literally a deadweight; he also had to be capable of working hard over short periods, in nerve-racking and unsavoury conditions; he had to operate as a member of a highly organised team, for squabbles at a

Tomb robbers in action

graveside over who did what, were hardly conducive to a successful corpse extraction. He should have no moral scruples or be handicapped by superstitions of any sort, nor should he feel any revulsion at having to handle cold yielding flesh (the shrouds were left in the empty coffins). As corpses had to be tied in a doubled-up position in order to be put in the sacks, a good knowledge of knots was absolutely vital.

An eye for detail could be of paramount importance, even in the darkness of a graveyard, for he had to leave everything exactly as he found it (except the body!). Digging being thirsty work, the ability to hold his liquor – and then his tongue – was indispensable and, if he was a gang leader, he should not be overly generous when it came to rewarding his subordinates.

Before going on ops., military-style information was vital and so agents would be necessary to notify him about recent burials and also of the enemy's' possible defences. For a price he would be informed of imminent or actual deaths by undertakers and their assistants, doctors, poorhouse keepers and nurses. Others in equally strategic, albeit more menial, posts were invaluable; grave diggers of course, many of whom filled graves during the daytime and then, either directly or indirectly, helped to empty them at night; men employed as cemetery watchmen who would leave gates unlocked and look the other way at the right moment; sextons, grooms and porters, even barmen and barmaids whose information after overhearing a snatch of conversation, or awareness of rooms being booked in their tavern for a funeral wake, would thereby contribute to the snatch of a body. Itinerants such as tramps, pedlars and down-and-outs who noticed a funeral taking place would always be recompensed for the information.

While en route to or from a tavern, should they happen to notice a funeral procession, they would adopt a solemn mien and join the cortege. On arrival at the cemetery they would note the position of the grave and return, suitably equipped, later that evening. Similarly, a quick-witted body snatcher, upon witnessing someone in the street collapse with a fatal heart attack or similar, would immediately feign shock and distress over the unexpected death of his 'cousin', claim the corpse, attend the inquest, then deliver the cadaver to his eagerly awaiting customer! Others, equally ingenious, played a dual role; by night body snatchers, by day undertakers' assistants! The poet Tom Hood in his *Poetical Works* penned verses which summed up the grim charade;

'By day it was his trade to go, sending the black-coach to and fro,
And sometimes at the gate of woe, with emblems suitable,
He stood with brother mutes to show, that life is mutable.
But long before they passed the ferry, the dead that he had helped to bury,
He sack'd (he had a sack to carry the bodies off in),
In fact he let them have a very short fit of *coffin*!'

Indeed some undertakers themselves were unscrupulous enough to co-operate with the resurrection men (at a price of course) to the extent of removing the corpse from the coffin after the relatives had bade their tearful farewells, then filling the coffin with a sufficient weight of sand prior to the funeral service. This arrangement suited the body snatchers perfectly, eliminating as it did the need for digging the cadaver up, and the concomitant risk of detection or worse.

Prior to a raid on a previously unvisited cemetery, the body snatcher would need to reconnoitre the area for possible hazards, ascertain approach and escape routes for his vehicle, usually a gig (a fast, two-wheeled one-horse carriage without a hood, sometimes fitted with rubber tyres, the horse's hooves being bound with a similar material to maintain silence), assess gateways and wall heights, the proximity of the nearest dwellings, the existence of any police or vigilante patrols and, if so, the times and duration of their duty. And, depending on the time of year, the hours of dusk and dawn and the phases of the moon.

As in any profession, he and his gang members had to have the correct clothing and equipment for the job; a vehicle of the type already described; smocks to wear, winter or wet-weather body snatching being a muddy business; spades, of course, incorporating wooden blades to avoid making clicking sounds on striking a stone; a dark lantern (a type fitted with a sliding shutter to direct its light only where required); groundsheets; crowbars, ropes and hooks; sacks in which to carry the bodies and straw to cover them in the gig, and perhaps a ladder with which to gain entrance to high-walled cemeteries.

On rare occasions a firearm of some description was carried, not always for defence as exemplified by a report in an Irish newspaper in February 1830 headed 'Desperate Engagement with Body Snatchers' and going on to describe how 'The remains of the late Edward Barrett Esq., having been interred in Glasnevin churchyard on the 27th of last month, persons were appointed to remain in the churchyard all night to protect the corpse from the sack-em-up gentlemen' and it seems the precaution was not unnecessary for 'on Saturday night last, some of the gentry made their appearance but soon decamped on finding they were likely to be opposed'. Nothing daunted however, they returned on Tuesday morning with augmented force, and well armed. 'About ten minutes after two o'clock, three or four of them were observed standing on the wall of the churchyard, while others were endeavouring to get on it also. The party in the churchyard warned them off and were replied to by a discharge from firearms. This brought on a general engagement; the sack-em-up gentlemen fired from behind the churchyard wall, by which they were defended, while their opponents on the watch fired from behind the tomb-stones. Upwards of 58 to 60 shots were fired. One of the assailants was shot – he was seen to fall and his body was carried off by his companions. Some of them are supposed to have been severely wounded, as a great quantity of blood was observed outside the churchyard wall, notwithstanding the ground was covered with snow. During the firing, which lasted for upwards of a quarter of an hour, the church bell was rung by one of the watchmen which, with the discharge from the firearms, collected several of the townspeople and the police to the spot, several of the former, notwithstanding the severity of the weather, in nearly a state of nakedness; but the assailants were by this time defeated, and effected their retreat. Several of the head-stones bear evident marks of the conflict, being struck by the balls, etc.'.

The horrified reactions of any local community upon discovering that their parish cemetery had been raided, perhaps more than once, can best be exemplified by a report in a book *Doings in London* published in 1828, describing the riots which took place in Lambeth in 1795. 'Twenty of the parishes of the metropolis and its neighbourhood coalesced to prevent the robbery of graveyards, the committee setting forward as a reason the dreadful scene that had just taken place in Lambeth burial-ground. One night three men were discovered conveying away five human bodies in three sacks. In consequence of this, people of all descriptions, whose friends had recently been buried there, assembled on the ground the next morning and demanded to be allowed to examine the graves. This being refused, a furious contest took place between the populace and the peace-officers, who were soon overpowered. The assailants now rushed into the burial-ground and began tearing open the graves, when an immense number were found to be empty. Many of the people, in a kind of phrenzy, snatched up the empty coffins of their deceased relations and ran with them through the neighbouring streets'.

The committee proceeded to state that they had ascertained that the gravedigger was the chief robber and that eight eminent surgeons were in the habit of buying these bodies; that they had retained in their pay fifteen body stealers, and five shillings were given to the grave-diggers for each corpse they permitted to be taken. Thirty burying-grounds had been robbed. The surgeons paid for each adult corpse, if not green or putrid, two guineas and a crown; and for persons under age, six shillings for the first foot in length and nine pence per inch for all above it. One eminent quack, who styled himself an Articulator, was proved to have made a wanton use of these bodies by using the skulls for nail-boxes, soap-trays etc., and his child had an infant's skeleton to play with as a doll. The committee also stated that much of the human flesh had been converted into an adipose substance resembling spermaceti and burnt as candles (see the reference to 'Hands of Glory' later in this chapter) whilst some had been converted into soap.

Another occasion in which violence involved local vigilantes guarding their local cemetery was reported by a correspondent to a nineteenth century *Notes and Queries* magazine column. She described how, in 1824, when she was then twelve years old, her brother James joined with others, taking turns to hide in the church porch while guarding the grave of a recently deceased neighbour against body snatchers. He was on the early shift till midnight, but about 9 pm the writer, at home with her mother, heard a noisy disturbance outside and on going to investigate, saw her brother and a crowd of thirty to forty others approaching. James rushed into the house shouting 'Mother, where's that small poker? We've got the rascals and we'll pay them off!' His mother remonstrated but he took the poker and hurried off to join his comrades, who were dragging three men towards the village duck pond. After being manhandled and thoroughly ducked, they were held in the village inn overnight. Next day the writer visited the White Horse inn, where she saw the body snatchers 'their clothes torn, faces covered with blood and bruises and dirt'. They were later taken before magistrates and sentenced to twelve months imprisonment in Ilford Gaol.

This type of encounter was the exception rather than the rule. Other less desperate methods were adopted by those who wanted at all costs to ensure that their dead relatives were left undisturbed until Resurrection Day rather than being dug up and violated by the Resurrection Men. Some of the measures were simple, others more ingenious. But just as security devices in this century are never infallible, so none in that era was completely snatcher-proof. Fifteen-feet high boundary walls topped with carefully balanced stones offered little defence, being negated by the use of ladders and the body snatchers replacing the stones afterwards. Walls set with shards of glass or iron spikes were covered with sacking during the attack, or the sextons were simply bribed to unlock the gates.

Some local authorities installed spring guns which detonated when trip wires were activated, and these occasionally proved lethal. An example, detailed in Chapter 1, was the raid by medical students which resulted in one of them being fatally shot.

Had they been professionals, of course, the female gang members would have played their part in advance to avoid such calamities. Dressed in black and masquerading as distraught relatives they would visit the cemeteries and while grieving at the graveside, would either disconnect the wires or mark their position accurately so that their colleagues could do so the same night. The trip wires would be reconnected before the men departed, because it was essential that no trace of their visit should be left behind. Failure to observe this precaution would cause the locals to be on the alert in future, and that particular hunting ground having to be placed on the body snatchers' 'no go' list for some time to come.

Marble tombstones or heavy stone slabs placed in position over the graves were certainly a deterrent, but generally proved too expensive for ordinary families, as were 'mortsafes'. These iron cages or frames of various sizes and designs consisted of interlaced rods which, set in mortar, covered the grave completely, their necessary removal depriving the body snatchers of their most vital commodity, time. In some country areas Mortsafe Societies were formed, the members of which, in addition to paying a small annual subscription, also undertook to guard the graves for the necessary period. After being in position for about six weeks, the devices were generally removed as putrefaction of the corpse would have taken place by then. It was essential, of course, that corpses for the purpose of surgical demonstration and dissection be fresh.

Just as Mortsafe Societies were formed, so 'Watch Clubs' were organised in some areas, the conditions of membership being a pledge to do duty by watching in any churchyard where a member was buried. Mr John Gusthard related in the *Newcastle Weekly Chronicle* of January 1888 that: 'years ago I was appointed substitute for a member to watch in Cornhill Churchyard over the bodies of two men. So far as I remember'

Two types of mortsafe in Greyfriars Cemetery, Edinburgh

he went on, 'the watch-house, provided for concealment and shelter, was without comforts except for a fire-grate and coals. Two men were considered a staff, and each was provided with a blunderbuss, powder and shot, a kettle and frying pan being common to both. My companion, Johnson by name, was much my senior and, of course, my leader. We were instructed

An upright mortsafe in Greyfriars Cemetery, Edinburgh

to visit the graves with a dark lantern at intervals during the night, and I can say we did our duty punctual to the moment sworn. Nothing disturbed the tranquillity of the churchyard that night but the howling of the wind, and our weapons were never used'.

On another occasion he visited a family grave being extended to receive another relative and described how, on looking into the cavity 'I perceived the sextons were preparing against a fall. Some soil had already fallen and had laid bare about ten inches of an iron bar some three inches wide, which the sexton was striking with his spade, trying to disconnect it

DEVICES FOR FOILING BODY-SNATCHERS

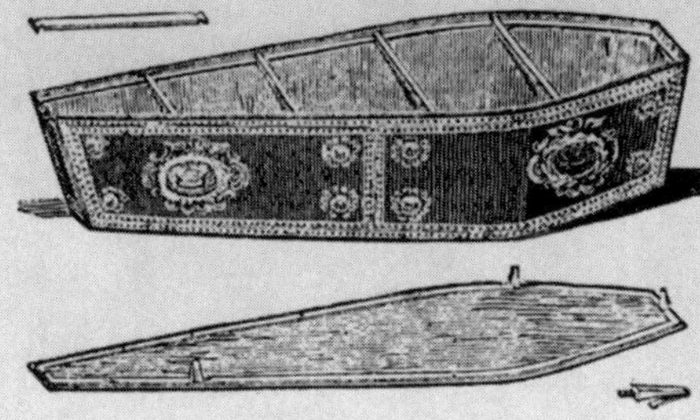

An iron coffin patented by a Mr. Bridgman in the first quarter of the nineteenth century. The lid had fourteen springs, and was laid over four dovetailed bars which stretched across the coffin. The springs caught under a bar which was riveted to the inside of the coffin. Cement was used to seal the lid. In *The Times* of February 24th, 1833, Mr. Bridgman defied the body-snatchers to open one of these coffins, which they failed to do

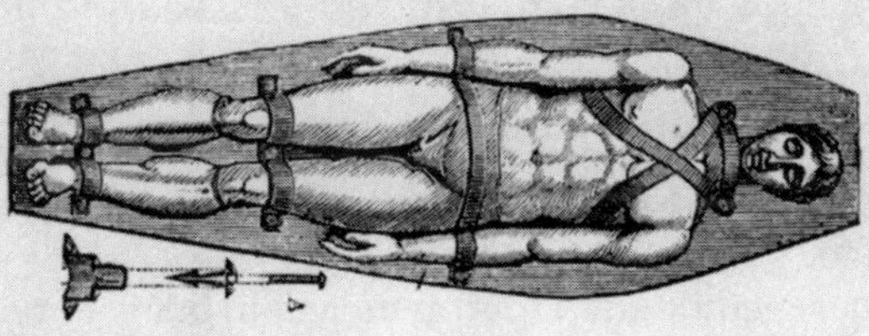

A device patented about the same time by a Mr. Hughes, whereby the body was secured to a false bottom in the coffin. The specifications also provided for an iron grating over the corpse

Snatcher-proof coffin made in iron instead of wood

a wooden spile (a heavy timber stake) which interfered with his progress. The spile was crumbling into dust, but the iron hoop on the top showed that it had been about three-and-a-half inches in diameter. This would have puzzled me had I not remembered my grandmother's stories about body snatchers. To defeat them my father had laid iron bars around the top and along the sides of the coffin to prevent it being broken open and the body drawn out. Besides spiles were driven into the ground to the level of the coffin lid, and an iron bar laid over

A putrefaction house in Crail churchyard: over the doorway is inscribed: "Erected for securing the dead, Ann Dom. MDCCCXXVI

all, was made fast to the spiles to prevent the coffin from being lifted entire'.

Another method used to stop the coffin being removed was to set strong stakes two to three feet long athwart the grave at intervals upwards above the coffin as the grave was filled in, or to fill the grave up with straw weighted down with a long heavy plank which in turn was secured to strong wooden stakes.

Visitors to some country cemeteries might notice not only mortsafes, but also small stone huts with thick wooden doors, positioned near to the entrance gates; these were built to house corpses, in their coffins, until they had decomposed, after which the bodies could be safely buried without fear of criminal exhumation. Above the doorways of some might be seen the inscription 'Erected for securing the Dead'.

A simple and, regrettably, almost useless method adopted, was to spread wreaths of flowers, shells or pebbles all over the newly made grave so that any disturbance would be immediately apparent. Alas this was easily circumvented by the wily resurrection men who, with the aid of their dark lanterns,

The Regency watchman's house, Old Wanstead Church, Essex

took careful note before starting work, and replaced them more or less in their original positions.

Despite all these defences, some of which seemed to be totally infallible, sometimes as many as a dozen corpses at any one time continued to disappear from graveyards. One method of extraction has already been described in the first chapter. Another, somewhat similar, entailed removing some feet of earth from above the head of the coffin, then thrusting a long iron rod downwards until contact was made. This rod incorporated a screw thread at its extremity and, when a long handle was inserted in the uppermost end and turned, the screw was driven deep into the wooden coffin lid. Next, upward pressure was applied to the handle by two or more men until the section of the coffin unsupported by the weight of

Wooler's British Gazette Oct 13 1822

MANY Hundred DEAD BODIES will be dragged from their Wooden Coffins this winter, for the anatomical lectures (which have commenced), the articulators, and for those who deal in the dead for the supply of the country practitioner, and the Scotch schools. The question of right to inter in iron, is now decided. Lord Chief Justice Abbott declared he wished they might be generally used. Justice Bailey declared, that if the Ecclesiastical Court was to grant a [illegible] for a fee, then, the Court of King's Bench would grant a prohibition, knowing it had no such right. Sir Wm. Scott, now Lord Stowell, decided and directed the interment without any extra fee, as this question was raised by an undertaker, those undertakers who have IRON COFFINS must divide the profits of the funeral with EDWARD LILLIE BRIDGMAN. TEN GUINEAS Reward will be paid on the conviction of any parish officer demanding an extra fee, whereby I shall lose the sale of a coffin. The violation of the sanctity of the grave is said to be needful, for the instruction of the medical pupil; but let each one about to inter a mother, husband, child, or friend, say, shall I devote this object of my affections to such a purpose? If not, the only safe coffin is BRIDGMAN'S PATENT WROUGHT IRON one, charged the same price as a wooden one, and is a superior substitute for lead. Edward Lillie Bridgman, 31, Fish Street Hill, and Goswell Street Road, performs Funerals in any part of the Kingdom; and by attention and moderate charges [illegible] the recommendation of those who employ him. Twenty-five private grounds within the bills of mortality receive them as done, from 7s. to 21s. Patent cast iron tombs and tablets, superior to stone.

Method of securing corpses to the bottom of a coffin

earth broke off. It was then necessary to secure a rope around the corpse's neck or under the armpits. This ghastly task was usually performed by one man, suspended head-first by his companions as he was lowered into the cavity, there to grope in the darkness for the body. It was then hauled to the surface and in order to do this without catastrophic results such as decapitating the corpse or mutilating the upper torso, it was found that a gentle rhythmic action rather than a violent pull brought the cadaver safely to the surface. Once the shroud or winding sheet had been removed and thrown into the grave, the corpse was tied in a doubled-up position by rope around its thighs and torso and dropped into a sack, to be dragged or carried to the cart and driven away as soon as the burial site had been restored to its previous untouched appearance.

Should it be a family grave or one with more than one occupant (or 'thing', as the bodies were referred to by the snatchers), perhaps due to a recent epidemic, the *modus operandus* varied somewhat. Earth was removed and deposited on the ground sheets surrounding the area until the first coffin could be lifted out, the others being removed in a similar fashion. The corpses were then extracted and the coffins lowered into the grave in their correct order before the earth was shovelled back in, thereby avoiding any grounds for suspicion, should the grave be re-opened for any reason.

Such was the aura of invincibility which surrounded these men who struck in the night and vanished ere dawn broke, that many theories about the actual method of just how they extracted the bodies were formulated. One such was postulated by Thomas Wakley in a memoir he had written in 1823 and which was published in the surgical magazine, the *Lancet*, in 1896. In it he surmised that in order to avoid disturbing the appearance of the grave the body snatchers would actually start fifteen or twenty feet away from either end of the grave and remove a patch of turf about eighteen or twenty inches square. This he would carefully put by, and then commence to mine (dig down at an angle). 'Most pauper graves,' he continued, 'were of the same depth so, taking a five-foot deep grave, the coffin lid would be about four feet from the surface. A rough slanting tunnel some five yards long would therefore have to be constructed so as to impinge exactly on the end of the coffin, which would then be lugged up by hooks to the surface, or the end broken off with hooks while still in the shelter of the tunnel and the scalp or feet of the corpse secured and the body pulled out, leaving the coffin intact and unmoved. The body once obtained, the narrow shaft was easily filled up and the sod of earth accurately replaced. Relatives, seeing the grave mound undisturbed, would seldom notice the neatly-placed square of turf some feet away'.

Mr Wakley's theory was ingenious and his engineering mathematics might well have been correct, but long after the *Anatomy Act* had made all the resurrection men redundant, one of them derided such speculations. This method was particularly impractical, he said, as it involved digging down into old, compressed earth, rather than the soil which the grave-digger had previously loosened. Digging straight down to the head of the coffin, breaking off the end of the lid by crowbar, hooks or screw, extracting the 'thing', then covering one's traces, was much the accepted strategy.

Some innovative coffin makers realised that if wooden coffins could be so relatively easy to break into, why not manufacture iron ones? An advertisement for just such a model appeared in *Wooler's British Gazette* on 13 October 1822, announcing: 'Many hundred dead bodies will be dragged from their wooden coffins this winter for the anatomical lectures which have just commenced, for the articulators, and for those who deal in the dead, for the supply of country practitioners and the Scotch schools. The violation of the sanctity of the grave is said to be needful for the instruction of the medical pupil, but let each one about to inter a mother, husband, child or friend, say to themselves, shall I devote the object of my affection to such a purpose; if not, the only safe coffin is Bridgman's Patent wrought-iron one, charged the same price as a wooden one, and is a superior substitute for lead. Edward Lillie Bridgman of 34 Fish Street Hill and Goswell Street Road, performs funerals in any part of the Kingdom and by attention to moderate charges insures the recommendation of those who employ him'.

As mentioned in the advertisement, lead coffins were also on the market, the lids of which were then soldered down. The same end was achieved in the Bridgman version which had interior spring catches that locked when the lid was placed in position. A Mr Hughes devised a way of preventing the corpse from being pulled out even if the coffin lid was broken open; his method involved metal straps which were secured across the body at intervals from neck to ankles, held tightly in place by special screws which fixed them to a false floor base.

Some of these 'improved' models were actually made and sold before it was realised by the church authorities that, unlike the wooden versions, these would never rot away, and the result would be cemeteries packed full with metal containers and their internal fittings. They were also probably disliked by the undertakers, the weight factor requiring additional pall-bearers and maybe even stronger springs on the hearses.

One technically-minded citizen of Dundee decided that if he couldn't deter the body snatchers, he would at least reduce their numbers; accordingly, as a Dundee newspaper reported 'he caused a small box, inclosing some deathful apparatus, communicating by wires with the four corners, to be fastened on the top of the coffin. Immediately it was lowered into the earth, a large quantity of gunpowder was poured into the box and the hidden machinery put into a state of readiness for execution. The common opinion was, that if anyone attempted to raise the body, he would be blown up. The sexton seemed to dread an immediate explosion, for he started back in alarm after throwing in the first shovelful of earth'. Who can blame him?

The fact that the shroud and winding sheets were always left behind in the coffin was due to a misconception. Other than a statute of James I making it a felony to steal a body for the purpose of witchcraft, there was no law against taking a body for dissection; there was no legal property in a body, no-one owned it, and so at that time the resurrection men believed that they had committed no offence in removing a corpse, but could be charged with theft had they taken the coffin clothes. In fact little action was taken by the law, the courts usually being excessively lenient; the only punishment, though one much feared by the resurrection men, was that meted out by the public. The gangs, of course, made every attempt to avoid their outraged reaction by working as quickly as possible at their nefarious task. Depending on the lightness of the soil, the depth of the coffin, the solidity of its lid, the size and weight of the corpse and other factors, bodies could be exhumed in anything between twenty minutes and an hour and a half, the former being achieved where the grave was shallow and the earth loose and without stones. If much gravel had to be dug out, the body snatchers adopted a way of throwing it out of the grave with a minimum of noise, probably by scattering it with a spraying motion of the spade.

The easiest, though not altogether risk-free part of the operation, was conveying and delivering the body. Occasionally a body snatcher, working independently, would dispense with a sack but instead would swathe the body in a large square of green baize of the type commonly used by street-porters. Concealing the bundle in bushes nearby, he would collect it the next morning and, casually carrying it on his shoulders, would deliver it to his customer the following morning. Where a gang was involved, perhaps even with more than one body as booty, a gig was usually used, but sometimes the vehicle was a cart, in which the bodies were concealed beneath bundles of kindling or heaps of vegetables. Corpses were almost invariably held in storage overnight, customer deliveries to local surgeons taking place the next day; others were despatched to surgical schools in Liverpool or Edinburgh, Glasgow or Oxford, Birmingham, Bristol or Exeter, the bodies being crammed into barrels and boxes, trunks and hampers, labelled as pork, fish, apples or even agricultural equipment.

Most were delivered safely although there were exceptions, of course. One noteworthy one occurred when three oil-casks labelled 'Bitter Salts' and addressed to a Mr G. Ironson of Edinburgh, awaiting shipment to that city from Liverpool docks on 9 October 1826, were found by the mate of the Carron Company's vessel *Latona* to be emitting such a foul stench that he informed his superior, Captain Walker. That officer inspected the casks and, on noticing a wisp of straw trapped by one of the bungs, he pulled it out – then stepped back as the stench became almost overpowering. With a sense of duty that can only be admired, he then removed the large bung entirely and inserted his hand into the aperture – to find his fingers encountering what could only be human flesh!

The law, in the person of PC Socket, was summoned and all the casks opened up. Inside were eleven corpses pickled in salt, the bodies of two women and one man occupying one cask, those of two women and two men in the second and of three men and one woman in the third. George Leech, the carter who had brought them there, was questioned, and he willingly led the policeman to the cellar in Hope Street from where he had earlier collected them. With the aid of a pickaxe, PC Socket's colleague, Constable Boughey, forced an entry and inside found soiled smocks, coats and trousers of the type worn by resurrectionists and syringes commonly used for injections into the veins and arteries of those destined to be anatomised. Nor was that all, for in a further six containers, three casks and three sacks, no fewer than twenty-two more bodies were found, those of nine men, five women, five boys and three girls, packed tightly together. Those in the casks had already been prepared for shipment, first by being thoroughly pickled in strong brine, then packed in the casks in dry salt.

Post mortems performed by a surgeon, Mr Thomas William Dawes, revealed that all had died naturally and had obviously been exhumed from their graves within the last seven days. The body of one woman had its big toes tied together with thread, a practice among some families to keep the deceased's legs together for the sake of decency. The Liverpool coroner ordered that the bodies should be buried in the local cemetery, in the casks in which they had been found. This seemingly callous method of interment was evidently necessary, for it was stated that 'some of them are so putrid that it is extremely dangerous to handle them'. This factor was apparently also the reason why no attempt could be made to identify them.

Although a Greenock man named Henderson, believed to be the ringleader of those responsible, escaped capture, another resurrectionist, James Donaldson, was traced, charged, and sentenced to a fine of £50 and imprisonment in Kirkdale Gaol for twelve months.

The inland distribution service also encountered difficulties in delivering its goods at times. In April 1888 John Mackay of Newcastle related an exciting episode that occurred when he was a boy at school in the Scottish town of Linlithgow. 'One afternoon,' he wrote, 'a farmer's lad residing at Gilston, about five miles away from Linlithgow, saw two men with a gig taking some bodies out of a dunghill in a field. The boy ran off and acquainted his master, who at once got a horse and went after the body snatchers. They, however, had decamped. He then rode to Linlithgow and, finding the men with the gig at the west end of the town, shouted to the townspeople "Stop the gig! There's corpses in the gig!" One of the men jumped off and got clear away. The other drove on, the farmer following. The gig was stopped in the centre of town where the man was dragged out on to the road, and the people proceeded to vent their rage on him. At first they pulled up gooseberry bushes from adjacent gardens and thrashed him on the face and hands until the blood poured down them. The sight of the gore only increased the fury of the crowd. Shouts of "Kill him!" were raised, and an attempt was made to seize him so that he might be drowned in the loch. My father, who was chief constable for the county, interfered and by sheer strength saved the unfortunate man from the populace – not however without receiving some injury from flying missiles – and had him locked up in the gaol for security.

Meanwhile the horse and trap had been taken to the town cross and there searched. In the trap were found the bodies of a man, a woman and a child about six years of age. I well remember the manner in which the bodies were tied up. The lower limbs were lashed to the thighs and both legs tied to the body, thus giving the appearance of rotundity to each corpse, otherwise the body snatchers could not have stowed them into the box of the gig. The bodies were laid out in the Town Hall and were subsequently identified. They had been exhumed from a churchyard situated a few miles west of Linlithgow. The same night the crowd got hold of the gig and smashed it to atoms. They made a bonfire of the pieces and cut the harness and burnt it also.

The delinquent was locked up in what was called the "black hole" of the gaol, and such was the feeling against him that a man was caught in the act of putting sulphur into the ventilator of the cell with the intention of suffocating him. After this a strict watch was kept at the gaol. The authorities had to exercise great caution in taking him to Edinburgh to be tried. The man was sentenced to nine months imprisonment. Upon examining the dunghill at Gilston the day after the men were seen taking the bodies away, three more corpses were found which had been taken from the same churchyard. After that, a public meeting was held and arrangements made to have a regular watch on the churchyard. A watch house was built, and two men from the town, furnished with firearms, attended in the winter, from sunset to sunrise, while the same number of men from the country did duty in the summer'.

Such vigilantes were not always successful in defying the criminals. An entry in a diary for 1832 describes how, in a Bristol cemetery, an old man guarding a relative's grave had his fingers severed by the sharp spade brutally wielded by one of the sack-em-up men.

Such was the pitch of public alarm at times that perfectly innocent men were sometimes denounced as being body snatchers and even attacked. One ex-grave-digger unjustly accused of violating his own dead wife's body, lived in the Scottish Borders. When she died he complied with her dying request that she should be buried as economically as possible and with the minimum of fuss. Accordingly he ordered a coffin, carried it home and, having enclosed the body, put it in a cart. After nightfall, he drove to the cemetery in Dumfries and there he buried it. Unfortunately his past caught up with him, for he had once been accused of offering to obtain corpses for medical students, a charge never substantiated though it resulted in his dismissal. On hearing of the surreptitious way in which he had buried the coffin, the villagers' suspicions were once more aroused, many alleging that he had already sold the body to the doctors, and in order to clear his name, the man had perforce to arrange for the exhumation of his dead wife and so satisfy the authorities. In a letter to his son dated 22 March 1813 he wrote

> 'These comes with a sory hart to you, for I am in a poor stat Concerning the fals Repoat corncerning your mother fownerall, with Bringing the Corps away under night; which was hir Desire Before she Died, as my master was to Be intd. that same Day; and I got all things to my own mind with the help of God and my good neighbours, when I came to Dfrs. (Dumfries). Dear John, to prevent fauther Clamour please be so good as to go to Dr ________ and let him know what you are going to Do, and goe to G B and R M with my compts. and go to the grave, and be Coreful not to Brak the Coffen lid, and J O to tak of the lid and turn upe the Shete Before witness, and give them a glass, and I pay them at my Comming; and after go to ____________ at the prenting offese, and Case him to put out a pareaft (paragraph?) in his Courreer (Courier) Conserning the fals report that is rummoring in the Country, and he whou Can be found any mor Shall be punched according to law. Der John, I am sorry for you and Sally. Do what you Cane to mak all right to stop the meletious (malicious) tongwes of the Sons of Beliell. So no mare present from your Degected father .... J B'.

Another, similar, incident occurred on 29 June 1823 in Edinburgh when a coach containing an empty coffin was seen proceeding along the south bridge. Suspecting that it either contained a body stolen from some graveyard or was en route to obtain one, a mob gathered and attacked the coach. Police called to the scene managed to protect the driver and his colleague, but the vehicle was dragged away, the coffin removed, the horses unhitched. The mob then trundled the coach through the streets until they reached the hillside. Once there, they pushed it over and followed it down, then proceeded to make a bonfire of the shattered wreckage, celebrating their victory by dancing round it. But their victory was as hollow as the coffin for the coach had been delivering it to a nearby house, the residence of a physician who had just died.

CHAPTER THREE

LONDON'S RESURRECTION MEN

Body snatchers operated throughout the country, wherever there were cemeteries to be raided, but naturally the centre of the trade was London where, in order to supply so many surgical schools, business was brisk. The major players were the top surgeons of the day on one side and the leaders of the gangs on the other. Two men and a woman have the dubious privilege of being the first to be prosecuted for this heinous crime. It all started in October 1777, when the remains of more than twenty dead bodies were discovered in a shed in Tottenham Court Road, London. It was concluded that they had been deposited there awaiting delivery to surgeons.

Investigations into this case revealed that the villains were John Holmes, a gravedigger employed at St George's Church, Bloomsbury, his assistant Peter Williams and a female accomplice Esther Donaldson. Their involvement came about when a Mr Eustonson, together with other gentlemen, met Williams, who was carrying a sack on his back, accompanied by another person. Suspecting that there might have been a robbery, Mr Eustonson asked him what was in the sack, Williams replying that he didn't know, that 'he was a poor man just come from harvest'. His questioner then seized the sack and on untying it was astonished (to put it mildly!) to find the dead body of a woman, her heels tied up tightly behind her, her hands tied together behind, and cords round her neck which forced her head almost between her legs.

Although arrested and identified as Peter Williams, all

knowledge of him as his assistant was denied by John Holmes, who further refuted allegations of any missing bodies. However on seeing a recently disturbed grave, the police, by pushing a long bar into the mound, discovered a coffin only six inches below the surface and on opening it up, found it to be empty. Not only was another grave, that of a Mrs Jane Sainsbury, also found to have been violated, her husband later having the unenviable task of identifying her remains, but Holmes was detected in the act of trying to conceal several pieces of shroud which had been strewn around on the ground, and he was further incriminated when sacks marked E Ellis were found in his house, this name corresponding to that found on the sack carried by Williams.

At the Middlesex court of quarter-sessions for December 1777 they were charged with committing a misdemeanour rather than a crime, not having stolen anything, and were found guilty, both being sentenced to six months in gaol and, on reaching the last week of their imprisonment, to be whipped twice from the end of Kingsgate Street, Holborn, to Dyott Street, St Giles, a full half-mile. This severe chastisement was duly inflicted, being watched and applauded by crowds of approving spectators. Their female accomplice Esther Donaldson, without a doubt Williams' companion when he was apprehended, was found not guilty, this acquittal, according to the *Newgate Calendar* being 'much regretted, as no doubt remained of her equal guilt'.

Branding the body snatchers as the 'Baddies', then the 'Goodies', if they can be so called, were the surgeons who, in order to teach their students and consequently maintain their own income and life style, collaborated with the criminals, not only to the extent of paying their exorbitant prices, but even to paying their fines and supporting their families should their menfolk suffer the misfortune of imprisonment. Failing to do so might result in a total withdrawal of supplies of corpses in the future. Not all surgeons were unwilling pawns in the game; some of them played an active part in obtaining bodies, one of the most prominent being Sir Astley Cooper who was not only President of the Royal College of Surgeons, but was also unofficial patron and protector of the resurrection men. It was said that no man knew as much as he about their crimes and way of life and he actually declared to a Committee of the House of Commons that: 'There is no person, let his situation

The Tower of London menagerie about 1820

in life be what it may whom, if I were disposed to dissect, I could not obtain. The law only enhances its price and does not prevent the exhumation.'

He was so obsessed by the science of dissection that at St Thomas' Hospital and later at Guy's he would, and did, dissect any dead creature. He even dissected an elephant, procured from the Royal Menagerie at the Tower of London. It was transported through the narrow streets with much difficulty, a procession viewed with hilarious incredulity by the Londoners and, the carcase being far too immense to get into his residence, he conducted the surgical operations beneath sheets of tarpaulin in his backyard, mats and carpets being draped over the gates and fences to conceal his scalpel dexterity from the watching crowds.

The details of the patients he attended were carefully entered in his records and he was kept informed of their subsequent state of health by their general practitioners. When the patient eventually died, Sir Astley would go to any lengths to obtain the bodies of those he had found of medical interest and dissect them. His records show that in 1 June 1820 he paid two notorious body snatchers, Hollis and Vaughan, to drive into the country and retrieve the cadaver of a man upon whom he had operated some twenty-four years earlier, the details of the account being: 'Coach for two, there and back £3.12s; guards and coachmen 6s; expenses for two days £1.14 6; carriage of subject and porter 12s.6d; subject £7.7s; total £13.12s'. A bizarre character perhaps, but one equally dedicated and conscientious enough to want to assure himself of the accuracy of his original diagnoses – and sufficiently consistent in his beliefs and principles to declare that upon his own death, his body should also be dissected.

Another equally renowned surgeon who participated in many a body-snatching foray was John Hunter. While ordinary corpses were always wanted, deformed bodies or those of unusual stature were particularly in demand, the demonstration of their anatomical features being of greater value to the students – and of course to the body snatchers. So it was that when the Irishman Charles Byrne died, Hunter was determined to obtain his body. Byrne was literally a giant, standing about eight-feet tall, who made a good livelihood by exhibiting himself in London, and the account of how Hunter triumphed was told by Drewry Ottley in his *Life of John Hunter* written in 1835:

> 'Byrne, or O'Brien, died in 1783. He had been in a declining state of health for some time previously and Hunter, anxious to procure his skeleton, sent his man Howison to keep watch on his movements, that he be sure of securing his body after death. Byrne learned of this and as he had a horror of being dissected, determined to take such precautions as should ensure his not falling into the hands of the doctors (surgeons); accordingly he left strict orders that his body should be watched day and night until a leaden coffin could be made, in which it was to be inclosed, carried out to sea, and sunk.
>
> Byrne died soon afterwards and, in compliance with his instructions, the undertaker engaged some men to keep watch over the body. Howison soon learned this, found out where these men went to drink when off duty, and gave the information to Hunter, who forthwith proceeded thither with the view to bribing them to allow the body to be carried off. He had an interview with one of the party at the ale-house and began by offering him fifty pounds for his co-operation; the man agreed, provided his companions would consent, and went out to consult them. He returned shortly, saying that they must have one hundred pounds. Hunter consented to this, and

> thought the affair settled, but the men, finding him so eager, soon came back with an increased demand, which was also agreed to; then further difficulties were found, and larger and larger demands were made until, it was said, they raised the price to five hundred pounds!'

The money was borrowed to pay them, and in the dead of night the body was removed in a hackney coach, and after having been transported through several streets, was transferred to Hunter's own carriage and conveyed immediately to his house in Earls Court. There, fearing lest a discovery should take place, Hunter did not choose to risk the delay which the ordinary mode of preparing a skeleton would require; accordingly the body was cut to pieces and the flesh separated by boiling, the process tinting the magnificent skeleton a brownish hue.

London did not have the monopoly of determined and ingenious surgeons, of course. Edinburgh's Robert Liston was never far behind when a particularly interesting corpse was simply asking to be garnered, so when a country lad, disfigured by having an enormously enlarged head, died, Liston and his unscrupulous confederate an infamous body snatcher named Ben Crouch, set out on the trail. Their exploit is described in Lonsdale's *Life of Robert Knox*, published in 1870, which tells how the body was buried in an exposed cemetery on the shores of the Firth of Forth and for weeks thereafter was guarded at night by trustworthy watchers. The agents of many Scottish surgeons had tried to secure the subject but all offers of money were refused.

After many weeks the contest between the watchers and the resurrectionists was abandoned by the latter when, one evening at dusk, two well-dressed gentlemen, smoking their cigars, drove up in a dog-cart to the chief hostelry of the little burgh; they alighted and requested that their horse might be taken care of for an hour. The 'whip-hand' gentleman told the ostler that he expected a livery servant to bring a parcel for him, which could be put in the box part of the conveyance, to which the key was attached. They walked away, and in a short time a man in smart livery came to the stable yard, deposited a bag under the seat of the dog-cart, pocketed the key and walked off – 'a canny silent man, or dull o' hearing'. Presently the two men returned to the inn, ordered out their trap and trotted off at a brisk pace. The sharp-eyed stable boy could not help remarking that the man in livery was deucedly like one of the two men, and fancied he saw a bit of scarlet lining under the said man's brown overcoat. 'Haud yer tongue, Sandie', said the lad's superior, 'Ye're aye seeing farlies'.

While the unknown gentlemen were trotting homewards at full speed, the guardians of the hydrocephalic body were approaching their post of duty. As usual on entering the graveyard they looked at the grave to see that all was right; but to their astonishment found that it had been disturbed, nay more, that the coffin was broken and the body gone! What – abstracted in near-daylight? Impossible, yet true! The dog-cart gentlemen were indeed the depredators, and most expert ones too, for they had achieved something that had baffled the ingenuity of the most experienced resurrectionists of Scotland. Availing themselves of the twilight just before the watchers took up post, they succeeded in disinterring the body and carrying it off in thirty minutes. Two such accomplished artists, in their own line, as Liston and Crouch the world never saw before.

Despite the horrific trade in human bodies, the public, as usual, managed to inject a certain brand of humour into the subject. The poet Thomas Hood (1799-1845) composed the following whimsically pathetic ballad;

Mary's Ghost!

Twas in the middle of the night,
To sleep young William tried,
When Mary's ghost came stealing in
And stood at his bedside.
Oh William, dear! Oh William, dear!
My rest eternal ceases;
Alas! my everlasting peace
Is broken into pieces.
I thought the last of all my cares
Would end with my last minute;
But tho' I went to my long home
I didn't stay long in it.
The body snatchers, they have come,
And made a snatch at me;
It's very hard them kind of men
Won't let a body be!
You thought that I was buried deep,
Quite decent-like and chary,
But from her grave in Mary-bone
They've come and boned your Mary.

The arm that used to take your arm
Is took to Dr Vyse
And both my legs are gone to walk
The Hospital at Guy's.
I vow'd that you should have my hand,
But fate gives us denial;
You'll find it there at Dr Bell's
In spirits and a phial.
As for my feet, the little feet
You used to call so pretty,
There's one I know, in Bedford Row,
The t'other's in the City.
I can't tell where my head is gone,
But Dr Carpue can;
As for my trunk, it's all pack'd up
To go by Pickford's van.
I wish you'd go to Mr P.
And save me such a ride;
I don't half like the outside place
They've took for my inside.
The cock it crows – I must be gone!
My William, we must part!
But I'll be yours in death, altho'
Sir Astley has my heart.
Don't go to weep upon my grave
And think that there I be;
They haven't left an atom there
Of my anatomie.

The identity of Dr Vyse is unknown; Dr Bell was anatomy lecturer at the Middlesex Hospital; Bedford Row was the street in which a Dr Abernethy lived; 'in the City' referred to the Aldersgate City School of Anatomy; Dr Joseph Carpue was the head of an important private school of anatomy in Dean Street, Soho; Mr P was Richard Partridge, demonstrator of anatomy at King's College Hospital, and Pickfords was the renowned furniture removal firm.

But who were the evil men, these human jackals whose nefarious activities gave rise to such macabre verses? Of the several gangs operating in London in the early years of the nineteenth century one gang, a leading member of which was Joseph Naples, dominated the body-snatching scene. He was born in Deptford, London, in 1774, the son of a respectable stationer and bookbinder, and was given a good education. That his reading and writing were above the average was evidenced by his diary, a record he meticulously kept for over a year which, had it fallen into the hands of the authorities, would have provided them with highly incriminating evidence against him and his fellow gang members.

When old enough, he joined the Royal Navy, being listed in the muster-book of HMS *Excellent* in 1797 as an Able Seaman, and he was a member of the crew when that warship was engaged in the naval action which took place off Cape St Vincent in that year. When the fleet returned to England he proceeded to squander his prize money (the spoils of war, proceeds from the capture and looting of enemy vessels divided proportionally between members of the ship's crew in proportion to their rank) and enlisted in a ship cruising in Channel waters. Deserting from that vessel, he took a job as gravedigger in Spa Fields cemetery, London. While thus employed he made the acquaintance of a Scotsman named White who, being engaged in the marketing and supply side of the gruesome business, persuaded him to supplement his meagre council wages by becoming a body snatcher.

At first squeamish at the prospect of also having to steal the bodies of babies, he soon overcame his scruples and disinterred any corpse that would bring him a good return, employing an ingenious method of his own devising. When the mourners had departed from the cemetery he would lower himself into the grave, remove the body from the coffin and place it in a sack before starting to fill up the grave around it; he would then repeatedly reposition the sack on top of the earth he was gradually replacing, until it was nearing the level of the surface, finally covering it with an inch or two of soil, thereby leaving it ready to be collected after dark with a minimum of exertion.

But Nemesis overtook Naples when White was arrested for being in possession of a corpse and, although the Scotsman escaped, positive identification of the corpse proved not only that the body had been stolen from Spa Fields cemetery, but further investigation revealed that other graves there contained only empty coffins. As this could only have happened with the connivance of the gravedigger, Naples was taken into custody and eventually sentenced to two years imprisonment. However, with the assistance of another prisoner he escaped via a skylight in the roof, finally gaining his freedom by surmounting the high outer wall by means of a rope.

Little love was lost between him and a confederate, Ben Crouch (of whom more later), each man being only too ready to betray the other to the authorities when tension between them ran high, and on the occasion of Naples' escape, it was Crouch who laid the information which resulted in his recapture. However judicial retribution was avoided by the intercession with the authorities of one of Naples' major customers, the surgeon Sir Astley Cooper. But Naples' continued activities brought him into further conflict with the authorities later on when he was caught red-handed in Woolwich cemetery. Again he was imprisoned, this time in Maidstone Gaol. Unable to escape, he whiled away the time by methodically compiling a record of his fellow felons, listing their personal details, their age, crime, occupation, duration of sentences, etc.

Despite his obviously criminal nature, he was described by another surgeon as a civil and well-conducted man with a pleasing expression of countenance and of respectful manners, an attitude no doubt appreciated by the members of the Select Committee on Anatomy to whom he gave evidence in 1828. As the most intelligent member of the largest London gang he had all the trade statistics at his fingertips and so was able to inform them that the production figures for 1809/10 were 305 adult bodies and 44 small (i.e. bodies under three feet long and classified as 'large small', 'small' and 'foetus', the latter being sold at so much an inch) disposed of in England, 37 being sent to Edinburgh and 18 left in stock, unsold. The figures for 1810/11 were 332 adults and 47 smalls, the average price at that time being four guineas (£4.4.0) each, although this varied widely depending on market forces and demands at any given time, sometimes reaching as much as £14.14.0 per corpse. When it is realised that in 1778/9 there were estimated to be over two hundred body snatchers operating in London alone, that figure excluding such 'sub-contractors' as informers, assistants and the like, the number of bodies and amount of money which must have changed hands showed just what a major industry body snatching had become.

Admitting to the Committee members his timidity in the face of the violence endemic to his profession Naples declared: 'I left in 1820; to be sure I did go out several times after that but then we had our men shot away from us and it was very dangerous; on one occasion a man was shot in four places and we took him away with us; to be sure, I had never gone out with him before and he was an incautious hand; he came and told us where the body was to be got, and we went with him'.

With the passing of the *Anatomy Act* in 1832 which authorised surgeons to obtain sufficient specimens from legal sources, Joseph Naples, like the others of his evil profession, immediately became redundant and obtained a post as a servant in the appropriate surroundings of the dissecting rooms in St Thomas' Hospital. Like so many of his kind, he was fond of his drink and this addiction eventually brought about his demise. The date and place of death is not known, nor whether his cadaver, if unclaimed by friends or relatives, thereby became eligible for dissection; but whatever became of his body, we must be grateful for his diary, affording as it does a fascinating insight into the day-to-day, or rather the night-to-night, lifestyle of the resurrectionists. So meticulous was he, that his diary even included a page on which were written out *The Rules for finding the Moon on any given Day* in respect of the years 1812 and 1813 – for bright moonlight was the bane of body snatchers.

In this unique document he recorded the events occurring during the period 28 November 1811–5 December 1812, the months May to June being left blank as no anatomy classes took place during the summer months. During the nine working months he and his accomplices carried out 95 successful raids, harvesting 456 bodies, an average rate of approximately 5 bodies per sortie being achieved. Their best night was 2 February 1812 when they dug up 19 bodies; 11 large, 5 small and 3 foetuses. Nor was this an isolated instance, the diary entry for the 20th of that month reading 'Met and went to Pancress (St Pancras, a parish church situated between King's Cross and Kentish Town); got 15 large and 1 small, took them to Barthol/w.' Nightly totals as high as these were probably due to robbing cemeteries which contained a large number of recent deaths caused by a local epidemic.

The work was perforce restricted to the hours of darkness – not that Joseph and friends spent the daylight hours catching up on their sleep; far from it, for if they weren't packing bodies in barrels for despatch to Edinburgh and other cities, they were, as mentioned earlier, 'looking out', roaming the district looking for burials taking place or, should they see a cortege or a funeral procession, following it to its destination in order to note which 'crib' (cemetery) it was being buried in, and the actual location of the grave. They had time off from work, of course, when the anatomical students took their summer holidays, and doubtless applied themselves to the other ways of self-employment adopted by the criminal classes of the day, as burglars, foot-pads, pick-pockets and the like.

But their usual daily recreation was to squander the money they received for their nightly labours on drink, Joseph's diary recording many such occasions. On 3 December 1811 he wrote 'Went to look out and brought the Shovils from Bartholomews.............didn't go out that night, Butler (another gang member) and me came home intoxsicated'. On the 27th of that month he complained that colleagues Jack, Bill and Tom, being drunk, were unfit for that night's job, and the sortie planned for the night of 24th February 1812 had to be aborted because 'Bill, Jack, Tom and Nat Ure Getting drunk, obliged to come home in a coach which prevented us going out to Harps (a cemetery)'. Given the high incidence of drinking among that particular fraternity, coupled with the need to get up at one, two or three o'clock the next morning in order to rob a cemetery, it is a wonder that they were even capable of holding the 'Shovil' the right way up, let alone exhuming the corpse and leaving everything apparently undisturbed.

Even when sobriety reigned, things went far from smoothly. It might be thought that robbing an isolated cemetery was a sinecure, but Joseph's diary endorses the deterrents listed earlier in the chapter by recording the hazards he and his accomplices actually encountered. On 27 November 1812 the sortie was a washout because he met the 'man with the lanthorn', i.e. the watchman, and earlier, on 26 August, he wrote that 'Jack (Harnett) and Holliss went to Islington, could not succeed, the dogs flew at us; afterwards went to Pancress, found a watch planted, came home'.

Occasionally they drew a blank through having been given wrong information and even when they had located the required grave and commenced digging, it was far from plain sailing; Jack Harnett was once nearly buried when the side of the grave caved in on him, his comrades having for a change to excavate a living body. Nor on every occasion were their efforts crowned with success, even when the corpse was finally extracted. Should it have been previously 'opened', subjected to a post mortem and so bereft of vital organs, it was no use as a specimen; similarly, if 'the thing was bad', i.e. if putrefaction had set in, the body would be worthless, although undeterred by this setback, Naples and his cohorts would extract the 'canines', the teeth, and sell them to dentists for the benefit of their more affluent patients – 'false teeth' were becoming more popular and all plates were fitted with human teeth. Nor would the limbs and head, the 'extremities' as Naples called them, be discarded; these would be severed and sold as surgeons could still use them for instructional purposes.

Inevitably the body snatchers also ran the risk that the corpses they exhumed were infected. Naples, on 19 October 1812, described how he 'opened another whole but (it was) bad with the small pox' and so abandoned it, although three months earlier, having exhumed '1 Large Yellow Jaundice' he nevertheless did manage to sell it to a surgeon.

Even after having successfully dug up a corpse or two and then driven away, relaxation was out of the question. On one occasion the cart broke down, and there was always the ever present danger of being apprehended while en route to the storehouse in which the bodies were deposited pending delivery to the customers. On the 17th January 1812 Naples reported how they 'Went to the Hospital Crib & got 4, was stopt by the patrols, Butler, Horse & Cart were taken'. Their animals, of course, were particularly hard worked, having to pull loads at all hours of the day and night, so it was hardly surprising that, the 19th January 1812 being a Sunday, the poor beast wanted a lie-in, the entry in the diary complaining 'at home all night – Could not get the horse out of the Stable'.

But what about the rest of the body snatchers mentioned in the infamous diary, Ben, Jack, Bill, Tom and others whose names appear in this ancient record? Ben, surname Crouch, has already graced these pages in the account featuring the acquisition of the body of the 'Irish giant' Byrne by the surgeon Robert Liston, and also in his betrayal to the authorities of his colleague Joseph Naples. The son of a carpenter employed at Guy's Hospital, Crouch became a prize fighter, the not-so-noble art of fisticuffs being useful in his evil calling as a leader of a gang of body snatchers. Tall and powerfully built, his face disfigured by small pox, he was an intimidating figure, always flamboyantly dressed when off duty with gold rings adorning his fingers and valuable seals swinging from his watch fob. A bully and a braggart, he was offensive when sober and highly aggressive when drunk. On 'settling up' nights he ensured that the members of his gang drank to excess while he himself remained sober. Always on the look-out for other ways to make money, he once stole some cloth from a shop in Watling Street, was caught and tried, but managed to have an alibi which was doubtless provided by his criminal friends.

During the Peninsular War about 1814/15 he and his partner in crime, Jack Harnett, became sutlers, men licensed to accompany the army in France and Spain to sell provisions to the troops. On the nights after a battle these human jackals would crawl out among the casualties, stealing the gold epaulettes from officers' tunics, rifling pockets, stealing rings and any other valuables. Even more horrific, they would pull the teeth from the mouths of the dead – and any still alive though wounded were quickly silenced. The teeth were brought back to England where they found a ready market, not only among dentists, as previously mentioned, but also for those who had faith in the belief that toothache could be avoided if they carried a dead man's tooth around with them.

Ben Crouch had two younger brothers, one of whom was also a body snatcher. For whatever reason he gave up that way of life and joined the British Legion then fighting in Spain, and was killed in action. It would have been the height of irony if, in the mud, blood and darkness of the battlefield, Ben had gouged out the teeth of his own brother.

With the fortune Ben Crouch had amassed, he eventually bought a hotel in Margate, lording it over his customers in great style, but when his exploits became known trade fell off. About that time his path crossed that of the Harnetts again when he misappropriated some property belonging either to Jack or his uncle Bill. In the court case that followed Crouch was found guilty and received a sentence of twelve months imprisonment. On his release all his old colleagues rejected him. With his power base gone and having squandered nearly all his money, he was eventually found dead in the garret he occupied in a tavern near the Tower of London.

Although teeth, limbs and sometimes heads were salvaged from bodies which would otherwise be rejected by surgeons as being insufficiently fresh, body fat was a commodity which could be 'recycled' and sold for profit by some body snatchers. The *Universal Spectator and Weekly Journal* of 20 May 1732, commenting on the arrest and trial of one such, reported that: 'John Loftus, the Grave Digger, committed to prison for robbing of dead corpses, has confess'd to the plunder of above fifty, not only of their coffins and burial cloaths, but of their fat, where bodies afforded any, which he retail'd at a high price to certain people who, it is believed, will be call'd upon on account thereof. Since this discovery several persons have had their friends dug up, who were found quite naked, and some mangled in so horrible a manner as could scarcely be suppos'd to be done by a human creature'.

The practice no doubt alluded to, was the use of human fat for the purpose referred to in Robert Southey's poem *The Surgeon's Warning* which contains the line 'I have made candles of infants' fat', and also mentioned in Shakespeare's play *Macbeth* in which the witches' cauldron was said to contain, among other ingredients, the finger of a birth-strangled baby. For centuries a macabre belief existed among the criminal fraternity of Europe that the severed hand of a man, preferably one who had been hanged, or that of a new-born baby, if prepared in accordance with ancient recipes, possessed special powers. This gruesome object, known as the 'Hand of Glory' was particularly 'useful' to thieves and burglars as it reputedly had the power to incapacitate members of the household being robbed and also to indicate the whereabouts of valuables by extinguishing itself when held over the place in which they were concealed.

There were various versions of the device but all required that the hand be converted into the form of a candle holder. One recipe stipulated that the right hand be severed before the flesh had withered away, and then drained of blood. Wrapped in a winding sheet, it was placed next to a pot containing dragon-wort before being bleached in the sun till the marrow melted. Following that stage, a candle of a corpse's fat and Lapland sesame had to be made, its wick being of the cadaver's twisted hair or of fibres from a hangman's rope. The fingers of the hand having been bent towards the palm, the candle was then inserted between the two middle fingers. The hand was held upright in use by the stump of its wrist or, if the candle had been inserted in the middle of the palm, by being held horizontally by its wrist in the same way as a conventional candlestick.

Another prescription called for the hand to be drained of

The 'Hand of Glory' was reputed to render householders unconscious while their valuables were being stolen

blood and dried in a pot containing salt and saltpetre. After being subsequently baked in an oven fuelled with fern and vervain, a herb used as a powerful charm, the fingers and thumb were each threaded with a wick made from five locks of the dead man's hair soaked in a mixture of fat from his body and that of a black tom-cat. The final ingredient was the reciting of the Lord's Prayer backwards.

Yet another variation was for the severed hand to be wrapped in a piece of winding sheet and squeezed to remove all the blood. It was then placed in an earthen pot with saltpetre, common salt, peppercorns and 'zimost' (?), all finely powdered. After being left in the vessel for fifteen days it was then exposed to the sun during the time of the dog-star until it became completely dried. If not dry, it had to be heated in a furnace, again fuelled with fern and vervain, to extract the grease from the hand, which was then mixed with virgin wax and sesame from Lapland to form a candle.

As a deterrent the evil effect of the Hand of Glory could be nullified by anointing the doorway of the house with grease composed of fat from a white fowl, blood from a screech owl and the gall of a black cat prepared during the Dog Days. Clearly this elementary measure had not been taken by the proprietor of the Old Spital Inn near the village of Stainmore one night in the 1890s when a woman sought shelter for the night. On being offered a room she refused, saying that as she needed to leave early the next morning she would prefer to stay in the barroom by the fire. Mine host, distrusting the woman's explanation, instructed the maidservant to stay with her, and later both women settled down to sleep. However the servant's suspicions were aroused when she noticed that the legs just visible beneath the woman's skirt were clad in men's trousers! Even as she watched through half-closed eyes, the traveller suddenly took a Hand of Glory from his pocket, lighted it and exclaimed loudly 'Let those who are asleep be asleep and those who are awake be awake!' Then putting the infernal device down on the table he went to the tavern door, opened it and called his accomplices to join him. At that the young girl bravely leapt up and, pushing him out of the house, locked the door behind him and rushed upstairs to rouse her master – but to no avail; the dreaded Hand had woven its spell! No amount of shouting or shaking would waken him or the other sleeping members of the household. Returning to the bar-room she seized a jug of milk which had been left on the table and, desperate to douse the candle flame at all costs, emptied it over the Hand. Instantly the flame went out, and from upstairs she heard the sounds of her master and the others as they suddenly awoke – the Hand of Glory had been defeated!

Another practitioner in body snatching circles was an Irishman named Murphy who operated in the business in the

1820s, taking over after Crouch had left the scene. Possessing the obvious qualifications essential to his profession, he was powerfully built and entirely ruthless even with members of his own family. Suspecting his son of robbing him of some money, Murphy didn't hesitate to have him committed to Horsemonger-lane Prison, and such were the appalling conditions there that the lad lost his reason; when released he was transferred to Guy's hospital but died later, never having recovered from his mental instability.

In his overwhelming greed for money, Murphy was prepared to take risks, accepting them with equanimity even when, on one occasion while clambering over a cemetery wall, he was wounded by a charge of shot from a blunderbuss. Despite these occupational hazards, the jobs paid well; a sale of six bodies to one surgical school brought him seventy-two pounds, and later that day another six cadavers brought him the same sum. Paying each of his underlings four or five pounds left Murphy with a neat profit of over hundred pounds – and there was always the next evening to look forward to!

The account book of the surgeon Sir Astley Cooper includes items such as 'Dec 1827 four subjects, two male two female, from Murphy, at twelve guineas each, £50.8.0; on 29 Jan 1828 paid Mr Cock to pay Mr South half the expenses for bailing Vaughan from Yarmouth and going down, £14.7.0; 6 May paid Vaughan's wife 6s.0; 29 May paid Vaughan for 26 weeks confinement (in prison) at 10s. per week, £13.' One considerable outlay was £130, paid to get Murphy out of gaol in order that the surgeon could continue receiving the bodies necessary to supplement his teaching programme.

If, as mentioned earlier, a surgeon did not support and subsidise his supplier and family in times of hardship – or when sentenced to hard labour in prison – no further specimens would be delivered. Nor was that all; some gang leaders, Murphy included, demanded 'finishing money' at the end of an academic season. Records show that on 10 May 1827 one surgeon paid Hollis, Vaughan and Llewellyn finishing money amounting to £6.6.0, and two years later, on 18 June 1829, Murphy, Wildes and Naples also demanded and received the same amount for work previously done and paid for. Further financial pressure was exerted at the start of the lecturing season later in the year, retaining fees of fifty pounds or more having to be paid for his supplier's allegedly 'exclusive' services; should these payments not be forthcoming, disasters would follow. No bodies would be delivered, or the premises would be broken into and any obtained from other sources either rendered unusable by being cut up, or stolen to be sold elsewhere. If unable to effect an entrance into the premises, the gang would inform the police anonymously that a stolen body was in a certain dissection theatre.

This actually happened to Joshua Brookes in whose school that day lay a corpse for which he had paid 16 guineas. Not only was the body confiscated but the police officer conducting the search was presented with a silver staff paid for by a collection among the public. Brookes' determination not to pay the gang's high prices brought him nothing but trouble as when, on refusing to pay a 5 guinea retainer at the start of a season, two putrefying corpses were dumped near his school one night, one in Great Marlborough Street, the other in Blenheim Street, London. The hysterical reaction of the two young ladies who inadvertently stumbled over one of them in the ill-lit street can well be imagined; sufficient to say that had it not been for the speedy arrival of officers from the nearby Marlborough Police Court, Brookes would have been badly handled by the lynch-minded mob which had quickly gathered.

No measures were too unthinkable for body snatchers ruthlessly determined to extract their extortionate prices. Should a surgeon who required specimens with particular abnormalities not fall into line, they would wait until one such patient died, then spread the news around the city. Next, the corpse would be dug up, the deformed head or limb severed and removed, the maltreated cadaver then being left by the open grave to be discovered by the mob – with the inevitable results.

Another method adopted by the resurrection men was to pose as grieving relatives and incite the scandalised onlookers to attack the building by announcing that their deceased loved ones were at that very moment being butchered; within minutes windows would be smashed, surgical equipment wrecked, staff and students injured if the mob managed to gain entrance. A clear case of pay up – or else!

Murphy was also into the teeth racket. On one occasion, pretending to be looking for a suitable burial place for his dear departed wife, he gained access to a private vault belonging to a meeting-house. While inspecting it he surreptitiously slipped the bolts back on a side door, returning after dark to remove a number of teeth, acquisitions which eased any cash-flow problems he may have had, to the tune of £60! Another time, having discovered a private cemetery in Holywell Mount near Finsbury, he lost no time in making the acquaintance of the gravedigger, Whackett, bribing him not only for a duplicate key but also for information on those graves which would yield the most recently buried bodies. Six or more a night were then disinterred. Nor were any corpses that had deteriorated into little more than skin and bones left behind. After the teeth had been extracted, the remains were sold to articulators, men who were expert at stringing together the bones from various corpses to construct skeletal specimens. These were bought for a nominal sum by students for their personal study. Even as recently as 1938, plastic models not being available, a top quality skeleton, i.e. one with a flexible spine and with each bone clearly named, could be legally bought for about £15 and a skull for £2, although the cost of a top quality one, mounted and in a case, would be the same as an originally complete skeleton. Should a piratically-minded student wish to display the traditional skull and cross bones, the total cost would have been £2.15.0, £2 for the skull, 15 shillings for the two femurs.

Intense competition always existed between gangs. Murphy's rivals, Hollis and Vaughan, discovered where their enemy was obtaining bodies from and, in order to take over the lucrative molar harvest if nothing more, they asked Whackett for the same facilities, delicately hinting that even gravediggers sometimes ended up on the dissecting table. At that, Whackett reported them to the authorities. The subsequent publicity incensed the general public so much that the gravedigger was pursued and, after being thrown by the outraged mob into one of his own newly-dug graves, narrowly avoided being buried alive. Although Hollis and Vaughan managed to escape and go into hiding, that was not the end of the bitter controversy, for Murphy eventually informed on Vaughan and had him committed to prison for two years.

Like Crouch, Murphy, selling bodies at between two and ten guineas a time, made a considerable fortune but invested much more wisely by buying property, and when he died his wife and child were comparatively well-off – although to avoid the stigma of his reputation his widow soon after changed her name.

Jack Harnett, a stout, red-haired scoundrel, aped his leader Benjamin Crouch to the extent of adopting the wearing of garish rings and ornaments, and embroidering his speech with the constant use of coarse expressions and foul epithets. As described earlier, he had visited the continental battlefields on tooth-looting expeditions with Crouch and it was on returning from one of these trips, accompanied by his daughter (who, one hopes, was left in a nearby town while he was at work), that on disembarking on the wharf alongside the Tower of London, Jack met a friend and, scenting more business, decided to send his daughter on home by herself. Accordingly he hailed a hackney cab on Tower Hill and told the driver to take her and the luggage to their home in Deptford. As the vehicle approached a tollgate near their destination, the coachman suggested that the girl could avoid having to pay the toll by getting out there and walking the short distance to the house; as she did so he realised she had forgotten the luggage, so with a flourish of his whip he took off at high speed.

Upon hearing of the loss Harnett was insensate with rage, for the luggage included a box which contained the battlefield yield of teeth which he intended to sell for at least seven hundred pounds! Frantically he contacted a colleague he was sure could trace the stolen canines. This was Holliss, mentioned earlier, a man who, originally a sexton, had priced himself out of his job by demanding too high a fee for his information services to the body snatchers who then retaliated by informing his employers. Losing his job, he subsequently entered the profession himself and in addition to working nights as a body snatcher, drove a coach by day. At their meeting, Harnett promised him not only a hundred pounds reward for the recovery of the teeth, but also the cancellation of a judgement for eighty-three pounds he had previously instituted against Holliss.

Meanwhile the coachman discovering that the luggage contained hundreds of teeth and not knowing how to dispose of them, and aware of his fellow coachman's other profession, sought Holliss out for advice. Holliss, never one to waste an opportunity to make a quick profit at someone else's expense, shrugged his shoulders and, declaring that the teeth were almost worthless, nevertheless offered to take them off his friend's hands for a fiver! The offer being accepted, he then sold them to dentists around town in batches of twos and threes, and proceeded to celebrate his good fortune. News of the double-cross reaching Harnett's ears, the body snatcher informed the police that Holliss had been selling human remains and, accompanied by two constables, led them to the cab rank at the Elephant and Castle, where Holliss was arrested. At his trial in Croydon Holliss escaped judgement owing to a flaw in the evidence, but on being discharged found that Harnett had pursued the eighty-three pound debt and had sequestrated all his belongings, furniture, coach, horses, everything. Revenge was sweet indeed.

Even this disastrous result had little effect on Holliss' depraved character. Knowing that a horse had been stolen by a man named Page, he nevertheless bought it from him and resold it at a handsome profit. And when a reward of twenty pounds was offered by the owner of the stolen animal, Holliss wasted no time in claiming it by turning Page over to the authorities. Arrested, tried and sentenced to death, Page was executed at Horsemonger-lane Gaol, London. Such a vicious act shocked Holliss' colleagues, themselves no paragons of virtue, to the extent that they totally shunned him, and he died in poverty shortly afterwards. By contrast Jack Harnett's fortunes flourished; continuing to visit the Continent, he prospered to the extent that by the time he died at home in Deptford, he had amassed a veritable fortune of no less than six thousand pounds.

Jack's uncle was Bill Harnett, also a body snatcher but, in marked contrast to the average member of that calling, he was polite and eminently trustworthy, one surgeon describing him as 'thoroughly good-tempered and generally well-behaved; his language scarcely ever rude or offensive to anyone'. Loyal to his customers, the surgeons, he refused to increase his rates beyond four guineas per corpse despite pressure from Crouch, this ill-feeling eventually leading to violence between them. Bill, wiry and muscular, was also a pugilist, albeit a smaller man than his opponent, and although in the fight which took place on Wimbledon Common he did his best, he was no match for Crouch's bruising tactics, a broken jaw ending the unequal contest. Like his colleagues, Bill supped more than he should, his favourite tipple being gin. Rarely sober, he contracted consumption, eventually dying of the disease in St Thomas' Hospital. Such was the regard in which he was held by the surgeons that they willingly promised to respect his last wish not to be anatomised.

Drink was Bill Harnett's weakness but with gang member Vaughan it was his susceptibility to women that brought about his downfall. Not that he was teetotal, far from it, but he was basically unable to resist the opposite sex. A Welshman, he gave up his job as a stonemason's labourer to become a full time body snatcher, eventually coming off second best with Murphy over the affair at Finsbury cemetery. After that debacle he fled to Manchester and Liverpool and having his tools of the trade with him, proceeded to supply the anatomy schools of Edinburgh and London with bodies. Evidently missing his old haunts and drinking companions, he travelled south one Christmas, only to be picked up by the police who had been alerted by his arch-enemy Murphy. After trial and imprisonment in Maidstone Gaol he moved to Yarmouth, the bodies he exhumed from the cemeteries there being sent to the London schools of anatomy in barrels labelled as fish, to be collected at Billingsgate.

While living in Yarmouth he was attracted to a young lady and, neglecting to mention that he was already married, courted her. This preoccupation with romance resulted in his being reported, either by his wife or a rival, to the police regarding his source of income. Another spell in gaol followed and on his release he moved south to Devon, taking up residence in a house adjacent to a cemetery in the village of Stoke. There, in the guise of a retired gentleman, he invited two of his former assistants, together with their wives, to move in with him and his wife, the team resuming its activities, first exhuming the corpses virtually buried on his very doorstep, then operating further afield.

Life could have been idyllic for Vaughan had he learned his lesson, but it was not to be; unable to avert his ever-wandering eye from the damsels of the district, before very long he was making improper suggestions to a neighbour's housemaid. She however not only rejected his proposals but also informed her employer who, wrongly suspecting that Vaughan was a smuggler, reported his concern to the police. Unfortunately for our hero, a Bow Street police officer had recently been transferred from London to command the Plymouth force and upon investigating, immediately recognised Vaughan as a body snatcher.

To catch the suspect in the act, at the time of the next funerals, policemen were concealed in the undergrowth surrounding the cemetery. The plan was completely successful, the officers watching as Vaughan and friends exhumed the bodies and carried them home. Moving in, the Law searched the premises to find not only the corpses but, hidden in the kitchen, the shrouds in which they had been swathed – damning evidence indeed as such stolen property constituted a charge of felony. Arrested and found guilty in court, Vaughan was sentenced to seven years transportation to the colonies from where he never returned.

The 'Tom' of Naples' *Diary* was Tom Light, a body snatcher who only infrequently took part in graveyard activities. Previously a 'gentleman's gentleman', he had betrayed his employer's trust by stealing plate glass from the windows of his master's coaches, and following his release from the resultant seven-year gaol sentence served on a 'hulk', a prison ship moored in Portsmouth harbour, he joined Crouch's gang. On 13 October 1812 he was caught by horse patrolman Watts of the Hampstead and Highgate district and taken into custody – as were the three cadavers found in his possession, those of a teenage female, a young boy and a newly-born baby, all stuffed into one large sack and obviously just exhumed from a nearby cemetery.

At the hearing in Hatton Garden Police Court he gave his name as T Light, although he was also known under the aliases of John Jones and Thomas Knight. The police gave evidence that he had recently been indicted at Middlesex Assizes on a similar charge of grave robbing, but that he had evaded standing trial and so a warrant had been issued.

The resurrection man made a desperate attempt to escape from the courtroom but was recaptured; however his efforts were unnecessary, for evidence was given that the bodies had been taken from the parish cemeteries of either St. Giles or St. Pancras. But as these two burial grounds were separated only by a wall and because it could not be established which council could prosecute him, the case collapsed!

Despite the corpses being exhibited in the Elephant and Castle tavern in St Pancras, no relative came forward to claim them, and although it was finally established that the corpses were those of paupers and had in fact been interred in St Giles' Cemetery, it was too late to charge those responsible, Tom Light having already been discharged. The outraged reactions of the general public were reported in the *Sun* newspaper of

14 October 1812, the account adding 'and from the frequency of such offences, strong indignation was excited in the neighbourhood, from where a crowd attended (protested) at the police office'.

Two years later he was tried for a similar offence in the same court, the report stating that 'T. Light, W. Arnot and one named Spelling were brought up on Wednesday. It appeared that the prisoners were going up Holborn about half-past four o'clock on Tuesday afternoon, with a horse and cart. They were observed by two officers who, knowing the prisoners to be resurrection men, stopped the horse and cart and, after a hard contest, succeeded in securing the prisoners. They then examined the contents of the cart and found it contained seven dead bodies of men and women; one of the bodies was headless, but how it came to be so, remains as yet to be cleared up. They were packed in large bags and baskets.'

'The prisoners were followed by a large crowd to Hatton Garden Office,' the report continued, 'whence they were committed to prison, and the bodies were deposited in the lock-up house. The cart was hired at Battle Bridge. Some of the officers were sent to make enquiry at the different burial grounds. The Office [police station] was crowded with men and women who had some of their relatives buried on Sunday last, to see if they could recognise any of the bodies. The prisoners were brought up again on Thursday and discharged'. Such acquittals were not uncommon, those in charge of cemeteries being reluctant to come forward and thereby admit their negligence in guarding the property and its supine occupants.

Considered by his accomplices to be untrustworthy, Tom Light was 'blackballed' from that exclusive club, and became a horse dealer. Smooth-tongued, he managed to fool some of his Methodist relatives that he had seen the light and intended to earn an honest living. Having induced them to make a collection so that he could purchase a coach and horses and thereby allow him to go straight from then on, he promptly climbed up on to the box and proceeded to go straight – by departing for destinations unknown!

Another 'gentleman's gentleman' who eventually joined the ranks of the nocturnal spade wielders was William Millard, a man as much distrusted as Tom Light. Leaving his menial employment Millard became the superintendent of the dissecting rooms in St Thomas' Hospital, thereby being the recipient of the many bodies delivered there by London's resurrection men. Not content with his salary, he augmented it by paying for the specimens with his employers' money but then reselling them to the Edinburgh schools at higher prices and creaming off the profits, a procedure which enabled him to enhance his life-style to a considerable degree.

Upon his duplicity being discovered he was dismissed, and with the money he had amassed he bought an eating house in the Borough on the south bank of the Thames near London Bridge, though he still maintained contact with his friends the resurrectionists. Unfortunately word of his unsavoury associates circulated among his customers and his business declined to such an extent that he was forced to relinquish it altogether. With little prospect in view, he joined the ranks of the body snatchers, but alas for William, success eluded him again, for he was caught on a body-snatching foray in the graveyard adjoining the London Hospital. He was sentenced to three months in Cold Bath Fields Prison and in desperation appealed to Sir Astley Cooper to solicit a pardon for him, but to no avail. At this, Millard threatened the surgeon with violence, his dire predicament affecting his mind so much that before completing his sentence he died insane.

A fellow member of Joseph Naples' gang was Butler (first name unknown), a man who could surely have employed his indisputable talents to better effect. A short stout fellow with a happy-go-lucky demeanour, he was originally employed in the dissecting rooms of St Thomas' Hospital and it could be said that bones were in his blood, so to speak, for not only did he help his father, an articulator and dealer in bones, but such was young Butler's skill that he was employed to articulate the skeleton of the Tower of London elephant after Sir Astley Cooper had dissected the animal.

Not unnaturally he learnt a great deal about dentistry and at one period in his life was one of those who extracted teeth from the battlefield dead. Once, arriving in Lisbon during the war with Spain, he made his way across country and eventually reached the battle lines. It is reported that while there he met Sir Astley Cooper's nephew, Bransby Cooper, at that time a surgeon with Wellington's army, who asked him what his business was. 'Teeth,' Butler replied. 'How, teeth?' queried the puzzled medico, then no doubt looked horrified as his visitor exclaimed 'Oh, sir, only let there be a battle, and there'll be no want of teeth! I'll draw 'em as fast as the men are knocked down!'

Having acquired not only sufficient knowledge by those means, but also probably enough molar stock as well, he set up in practice in Liverpool as a dentist but, being constantly in debt through his dissolute ways, he soon absconded and headed for Scotland. It would seem that he joined the criminal fraternity there, for he was later accused of robbing the Edinburgh mail coach, a crime which carried the death penalty. Tried and found guilty, he was gaoled pending execution, but for some reason there was a delay in proceedings and, evidently bored by his confinement, he complained to the Governor who, on ascertaining the convict's legitimate pursuits, provided him with a dead horse on which to practice.

While engrossed one day in the complex task of stringing the bones together in their correct order, Butler was interrupted in his work by the visit of two foreign noblemen who were being given an insight into the English judicial system, the exalted personages being two Imperial Highnesses, Archduke John and Archduke Lewis of Austria. Highly impressed by Butler's expertise, they interceded on his behalf with the Prince Regent who diplomatically granted a pardon on condition that Butler left the country, never to return. So should any of the readers' ancestors have been reportedly adept in assembling the skeleton of a kangaroo - or bison - or giraffe ...!

Oddballs exist in every profession and body snatching was no exception, for Messrs Roach, Elliot and Parker stole, not bodies, but the lead with which some coffins were lined. Whether this was out of respect for the corpses they contained, or because they felt too squeamish to handle dead flesh is not known, but they certainly found a lucrative market among those who were prepared to pay good money for the lead, in just as do those criminals who strip church roofs today.

The Newgate Calendar reported the case of the three men concerned who dealt in lead, two being carpenters and, in modern parlance, the other a bent copper. The carpenters were William Roach and Robert Elliot who, while employed by a Mr Augurs to carry out repairs inside a church in Aldermanbury, London in March 1778, seized the opportunity to enter a vault in which was a coffin containing the body of a Mr William Thornton Aston, who had been interred therein on 1 January that year.

Stripping it of all the lead it contained, they took the metal to the house of a Mr Parker who, they knew, would give them a good price for it; as the going rate was a penny a pound and the weight was about 42 lbs., they anticipated receiving three shillings and sixpence. Unfortunately they had been seen by John Brotherous, an apprentice of their employer who, suspicious of their motives, some little while later decided to inform a constable he knew. As he approached the police officer's house he was surprised to see the suspects leaving, carrying empty sacks – and realised that PC Parker was not only a policeman but also a dealer in stolen goods!

On the arrival of other officers of the law summoned by Brotherous, a search of the premises was carried out. 52lbs of lead was found in Parker's house, the metal being identified as being of the type used in coffins, and some pieces, when reshaped, were found to fit the coffin shell in the vault. Final evidence of the carpenters' guilt was forthcoming when the name plate from the coffin was discovered in Roach's tool chest.

In court the defendants pleaded not guilty, their good characters being vouched for by friends, but the evidence was overwhelming; all were found guilty, Roach and Elliot being sentenced to three years labour on the Thames, incarcerated in a prison hulk moored in the river and working on shore under guard during the day, Parker receiving the same length of imprisonment in gaol.

Another sideline adopted by some body snatchers was that of stripping coffins of their fittings – the hinges and handles, screws and nails – though, of course, if caught the perpetrators faced the risk of being charged with theft of property. But when the metal artefacts were hammered out and shaped into 'cramp rings' there was always a lucrative market among superstitious people who believed that wearing such ornaments was effective in curing cramp, epilepsy, rheumatism and similar afflictions, especially if the metal had been in contact with, or near the dead. Usually the fittings were of iron, but more elaborate coffins sometimes yielded silver or copper, the latter metal even today being worn by arthritic sufferers in the form of bangles – though one trusts that the source is no longer a graveyard or church vault.

In his diary Naples mentioned the severing of extremities from an otherwise unsaleable corpse, and in addition to the arms and legs sold to surgeons, there was also a demand from those practising witchcraft and sorcery. So in order to cater for such fringe industries, some very small extremities were sometimes removed from the bodies and sold – thumbs, fingernails, little finger joints, knots of a virgin's hair and similar objects being considered absolutely essential ingredients for a witch's spell.

If carrying away lead, coffin fittings and limbs was not without risk, the successful conveyance of corpses called for many a ruse to be employed. You may remember the two students in Chapter 1 who pretended they were drunkenly singing and their corpse a drunken companion; luck favoured them, a toll keeper looking in failed to realise that what he heard was only a duet and not a three-part chorus.

Many anecdotes of similar occurrences were published in the broadsheets of the day. One a young man, returning from a tryst with his lady friend, noticed a cart parked by a graveyard, its sole occupant being dressed in a great-coat and slouch hat. He also observed that he – or it – sat very still. Realising what was afoot he jumped up into the cart and, finding his suspicions were correct and that the figure was indeed a recently exhumed corpse, he stripped the figure of its coat and hat, unceremoniously dumped the body by the roadside and, donning the clothes, took the cadaver's place in the cart. When the body snatchers returned from filling in the grave, each jumped up into the cart and took his seat beside the erect and silent figure sitting there. One of them whipped up the horse, which took off at a gallop, and in order to steady the lolling figure, the two men took hold of the arm nearest them.

After a couple of miles one of the resurrection men realised that the arm he was clutching was not as cold as he had expected. Turning to his accomplice he exclaimed, 'Why, Jack, the body's warm!' Then both gasped as the 'corpse' replied 'Aye – and I'll warm both of you in a minute!' With a shriek of terror both body snatchers leapt from the cart and ran, leaving our hero in possession, not only of a great-coat and slouch hat but also of a fine horse and gig, for naturally they were never claimed.

Another story involves a lover, but one lacking a happy ending. Two young Scotchmen, Ferguson and Duncan, were both in love with a Miss Wilson. Ferguson won her hand and heart but before they could become betrothed, he died and was buried in Buccleuch graveyard. His erstwhile rival, Duncan, promptly employed a well-known body snatcher who went under the pseudonym of 'Screw', the nickname given to him because of the dexterity with which he exhumed bodies (probably with the screw-bar used to break off the head end of the coffin lid), and together they went to the cemetery with the intention of digging Ferguson up and presenting him to Dr Monro, the local surgeon. However on their arrival they were dismayed to find a distraught Miss Wilson grieving beside the grave. 'However,' the story ended cynically, 'at last she went away – and the body of her late suitor was soon delivered to the college!'

Humour of a different sort was employed by a gang of body snatchers who happened to come across a drunk lying in the street. Seeing the opportunity to make some money without getting their hands dirty, they rolled him into their sack and, carrying him to an anatomist, promptly sold the inebriated gentleman. The sack and its contents were deposited in a cellar to await dissection the next morning. On regaining consciousness the victim frantically shouted for help. When the resurrection men returned with another body, the surgeon upbraided them for the deception and demanded what he was to do with his noisy guest. 'What are you to do?' they repeated. 'Why, keep him till you want him!'

As mentioned earlier, usually only summary justice was passed on those body snatchers unlucky enough to have some charge laid against them. John Mayall, in his book *Annals of Leeds* described how, in 1831, the body of Thomas Rothery had been stolen from his grave in Wortley cemetery. It was eventually discovered in the office of a solicitor, Mr Gaunt. It had been hidden there by the solicitor's clerk John Hodgson until the commotion had died down.

Hodgson was tried at Leeds Borough Sessions on 4 July on a charge of being in possession of a body with intent to sell it, and after a trial which lasted for four hours, was sentenced to be imprisoned in York Castle for just six weeks, and bound over to keep the peace for two years thereafter.

In the same year and town, the 'Courier' coach stopped to change horses at the 'Rose and Crown' hostelry and the driver, becoming aware of a nauseating smell previously dispersed by the slipstream, opened a wooden box among the baggage to find it contained the body of a man subsequently identified as a Robert Hudson of East Ardsley who had committed suicide by hanging. As no address label was attached to the box, it was not possible to trace those responsible, but the following year five men were arrested for a similar offence, one of them, a man named Teale, turning King's Evidence. All were found guilty and received prison sentences ranging from three months to one year.

Short prison sentences were certainly the order of the day. On Monday 29 December 1823 a Captain Hedley of Burleigh Street, Sunderland, whose ten-year-old daughter had been buried on Christmas Eve, wished to move her body to another part of the cemetery. On arrival at the graveside he was shocked to find the coffin empty; nor was that all, for the nearby grave of a two-year-old infant, buried at the same time, had also been desecrated and emptied by body snatchers.

As reported in a later edition of the *Monthly Chronicle* 'suspicion immediately attached to two strangers whose frequent visits to the churchyard, particularly at funeral times, had been observed; and one of them was apprehended that very afternoon. It was with difficulty that he was got through the streets to the police court room, for the mob which gathered, eager to take the law into its own hands, would have stoned him to death; and it was not until he was threatened with being handed over to the infuriated populace for summary punishment that he would acknowledge where he lodged.

On his at length doing so, the constables proceeded thither, and secured his accomplice too. Hedley's daughter's corpse was found in a corner of the room, covered with straw, but carefully packed up and addressed to Mr James Jamieson, Leith Street, Edinburgh. On another part of the package the address was Mr Alex Anderson, Leith Street, Edinburgh. A number of human teeth and some memoranda of the men's daily expenditure were also found in the room. It appeared from these that they had been about a month in Sunderland, and had during that time paid for six boxes, several mats and a quantity of oakum (rope) and twine; and as the body of Mrs Corner, aged forty-two, was the only one missing from the churchyard, in addition to the two already mentioned, it was presumed that their nightly visitations had not been confined to Sunderland, but had been extended into the country around, particularly as one considerable item of their expenditure was cartage (vehicles).

On the Tuesday morning they were brought before the magistrates and committed to Durham Gaol. One of them represented himself to be Thomas Thompson of Dundee, and the other John Weatherley of Renfrew – both names, there was reason to believe, fictitious. Tried at the Durham Sessions in the ensuing week, they were sentenced to three months imprisonment and ordered to pay a fine of sixpence each. The lenity of this punishment caused much surprise, and simply increased the popular alarm'.

The Monthly Chronicle went on to point out that the Sunderland churchyard was suitable hunting ground for the body snatchers because it was not overlooked by any houses and was close to the Town Moor. Besides, it was more than whispered that one of the parish officials was an active co-agent in such affairs. Further, one of the bellringers, a pipe maker by trade but who also kept a public house, had the reputation of being a regular body snatcher. Under such circumstances the friends of buried persons used to watch all night with lanterns, both in the Sunderland churchyard and the Gill cemetery 'where they might be seen from the road making their melancholy and weary round'. Whether their patrols prevented the horrific exhumation of any more cadavers was not reported.

CHAPTER FOUR

IN THE DISSECTING ROOMS

As mentioned earlier, body snatchers were obviously exposed to the diseases from which their prey had died, but by no means to the same extent as those who had to dissect the body and come into contact with the infected vital organs. This danger was colourfully pointed out by an anonymous naval medical officer who in an article published in Glasgow in 1829 described the typical dissecting room 'where, seated among putrefying corpses, inhaling the stench of dead bodies and exposed to the danger of losing health and life, the student toils thus anxiously, and in the midst of disagreeables unparalleled in any other course of study; while he perils his health by exposure to the pestilential atmosphere of a dead-house and endangers his life by braving the accidents too common to anatomists and which the experience of ages affirms to have been too frequently fatal ...' This account was far from exaggerated, for a number of students suffered and died in agony each year from diseases which entered their systems through minute scratches and cuts while examining the specimens on the dissecting benches.

On one occasion this ghastly result was brought about deliberately when 'Old Cunny', an Irish resurrectionist employed to supply bodies to the Ohio Medical College in Cincinnati, USA, became so incensed at the tricks played on him by the students that he delivered the body of a small-pox victim, thereby infecting many of his tormentors with the disease.

Perhaps even worse, psychologically, were the traumatic occasions when those present recognised the specimen as a friend or, even worse, a relative. One such instance involved body snatcher Holliss who brought the body of a child, a victim of scrofula, to St Thomas' Hospital in London. On being laid out for a preliminary inspection the corpse was immediately recognised by one of the students as his sister's child. The session was instantly terminated and, the shocked student having been attended to, the little body was taken away and buried, never to be disturbed again – one hoped.

The Monthly Magazine for April 1827 included a tale which might well have been factual concerning a sailor who, just having returned from a voyage, helped a party of his student friends to exhume a body and take it to the hospital. When it was removed from the sack, he was overwhelmed with horror to find himself looking at his sweetheart of whose death he had been totally unaware!

No doubt at all exists over the veracity of an event described by Dr F J Shepherd, formerly Demonstrator of Anatomy at the McGill University, Montreal, Canada, in 1919. 'I remember on one occasion,' he said 'a French student once finding that the body on the table was his late uncle. He said to me "What for you got mine oncle here?" I said I did not know it was his uncle; had I known it I would never have received him. I added that if he paid the expenses of removal, he could have him. He thought awhile then said "S'pose mine oncle come, s'pose he stay." And he did and was properly dissected.'

There were, of course, cases of mistaken identity, one of which occurred in the Border village of Cornhill in December 1830. A sexton, John Marchall, was awakened by loud knocking at his door and a frantic voice shouting 'Get up, Jamie! For God's sake be quick, man!' On opening it, he recognised the caller to be Robert, a young man studying medicine at the University of Edinburgh, the son of a local farmer who had recently died. Noticing the student's pale and distraught expression, he stared uncomprehendingly as the youth exclaimed 'Get your spade and mattock (a large pick having a wide blade used for loosening soil) and come with me to the churchyard quickly.' On seeing his obvious distress the sexton collected the tools and accompanied him. On the way, the student said wildly 'I'll be satisfied soon whether it is him or not. Think, Jamie, having your ain father laid out on the dissecting board for you to cut up. I had the knife in my hand when I saw it was my father. But I'll be satisfied before I sleep.

I left the hall and have ridden here, Jamie, to satisfy myself.' When his father's grave was reached, he took a spade and helped the sexton to dig the earth out. The coffin having been reached, he called out 'Break the lid with your mattock and put your hand in.' Marchall not unnaturally hesitated a moment, then slowly inserted his hand. 'Is he there, Jamie?' the lad enquired anxiously, then breathed a sigh of overwhelming relief as the sexton said reassuringly 'Aye, he's a'right. Naebody's fashed him, Robert; ye ha'e been mista'en'.

It must also have crossed the minds of many of the students themselves that should a fatal accident befall them, they themselves might well be displayed in front of their erstwhile colleagues for the better understanding of their craft; the possibility was certainly not lost on the surgeons themselves, their sentiments being expressed in Robert Southey's dramatic poem, *The Surgeon's Warning*:

All kinds of carcases I have cut up,
And the judgment now must be!
But, brothers, I took care of you,
So pray take care of me!
I have made candles of infants' fat,
The sextons have been my slaves,
I have bottled babies unborn, and dried
Hearts and livers from rifled graves.
And my 'prentices will surely come,
And carve me bone from bone,
And I, who have rifled the dead man's grave,
Shall never rest in my own.
Bury me in lead when I am dead,
My brethren, I entreat,
And see the coffin weigh'd, I beg,
Lest the plumber should be a cheat.
And let it be solder'd closely down,
Strong as strong can be, I implore
And put it in a patent coffin,
That I may rise no more.
If they carry me off in the patent coffin,
Their labours will be in vain;
Let the undertaker see it bought of the maker,
Who lives in St Martin's Lane.
And bury me in my brother's church,
For that will safer be,

And I implore, lock the church door,
And pray take care of the key.
And all night long let three stout men,
The vestry watch within,
To each man give a gallon of beer
And a keg of Holland's gin.
Powder and ball and blunderbuss,
To save me if he can,
And eke five guineas if he shoot
A resurrection man.
And let them watch me for three weeks,
My wretched corpse to save,
For then I think that I may stink
Enough, to rest in my grave.
The surgeon laid him down in his bed,
His eyes grew deadly dim,
Short came his breath, and the struggle of death
Distorted every limb.
They put him in lead when he was dead,
And shrouded up so neat,
And they the leaden coffin weighed,
Lest the plumber should be a cheat.
They had it solder'd closely down,
And examined it o'er and o'er,
And they put it in a patent coffin,
That he might rise no more.
For to carry him off in a patent coffin
Would, they thought, be but labour in vain,
So the undertaker saw it bought of the maker
Who lives by St Martin's Lane.
In his brother's church they buried him,
That safer he might be,
They lock'd the door, and would not trust
the sexton with the key.
And three men in the vestry watch,
To save him if they can,
And should he come there, to shoot, they swear,
A resurrection man.
So all night long, by the vestry fire,
They quaff'd their gin and ale,
And they did drink, as you may think,
And told full many a tale.

They looked askance with greedy glance,
The guineas they shone bright,
For the sexton, on the yellow gold,
Let fall his lantern light.
And he look'd sly, with his roguish eye,
And gave them a well-timed wink,
And they could not stand the sound in his hand
For he made the guineas clink.
And conscience late, that had such weight
All in a minute fails,
For well they knew, that it was true:
A dead man tells no tales.
Then, though the key of the church door
Was left with the parson, his brother,
It opened at the sexton's touch –
Because he had another.
They laid the pick-axe to the stones,
And they moved them soon asunder,
They shovell'd away the hard-prest clay,
And came to the coffin under.
They burst the patent coffin first,
And then cut through the lead,
And they laughed aloud when they saw the shroud
Because they had got at the dead.
And they allowed the sexton the shroud
And they put the coffin back,
And nose and knees they then did squeeze
The surgeon in a sack.
So they carried the sack pick-a-back,
And they carved him bone from bone,
But what became of the surgeon's soul
Was never to mortals known!

So not even those who paid the body snatchers were ultimately safe from them. It might be assumed though that some residual decency was finally shown to the fragmented remains of the corpses after having been dissected, by giving them a decent burial, perhaps in a communal or anonymous grave. Not necessarily so, for without going into the gruesome details it is only necessary to remind readers that so far as London was concerned, the river Thames presented an obvious means of disposal, as did the voracious animals housed in the Royal

Menagerie at the Tower of London. And according to the *Newgate Calendar*, the London surgeon, John Hunter 'had a well in the back part of his premises in which was thrown the putrid flesh, and with it, alkalis, in order to hasten its consumption'.

But there were happier, albeit very rare occasions in the dissecting rooms when 'dead' bodies were actually restored to life, as the following broadsheet, printed by Stephenson of Gateshead in 1824, so graphically describes. The preamble was entitled:

> **'MIRACULOUS CIRCUMSTANCE**
>
> Being a full and particular account of John Macintire, who was buried alive in Edinburgh on the 15th day of April 1824 while in a trance, and was taken up by the resurrection men and sold to the doctors to be dissected, with a full account of the many strange and wonderful things which he saw and felt while he was in that state, the whole being taken from his own words, as follows.
>
> I had been some time ill of a low and lingering fever. My strength gradually wasted, and I could see by the doctor that I had nothing to hope. One day, towards evening, I was seized with strange and indescribeable quiverings. I saw around my bed, innumerable strange faces; they were bright and visionary, and without bodies. There was light and solemnity, and I tried to move, but could not; I could recollect, with perfectness, but the power of motion had departed. I heard the sound of weeping at my pillow, and the voice of the nurse say "He is dead."
>
> I cannot describe what I felt at these words. I exerted my utmost power to stir myself, but I could not move even an eyelid. My father drew his hand over my face and closed my eyelids. The world was then darkened, but I could still hear, and feel and suffer. For three days a number of friends called to see me. I heard them in low accents speak of what I was, and more than one touched me with his finger. The coffin was then procured and I was laid in it. I felt the coffin lifted and borne away. I heard and felt it placed in the hearse; it halted, and the coffin was taken out. I felt myself carried on the shoulders of men; I heard the cords of the coffin moved. I felt it swing as dependent by them. It was lowered and rested upon the bottom of the grave. Dreadful was the effort I then made to exert the power of action, but my whole frame was immovable. The sound of the rattling mould as it covered me, was far more tremendous than

thunder. This also ceased, and all was silent.

This was death, I thought, and soon the worms will be crawling about my flesh. In the contemplation of this hideous thought, I heard a low sound in the earth over me, and I fancied that the worms and reptiles were coming. The sound continued to grow louder and nearer. Can it be possible, thought I, that my friends suspect that they have buried me too soon? The hope was truly like bursting through the gloom of death. The sounds ceased. They dragged me out of the coffin by the head and carried me swiftly away. When borne to some distance, I was thrown down like a clod, and by the interchange of one or two brief sentences, I discovered I was in the hands of two of those robbers who live by plundering the grave and selling the bodies of parents and children and friends.

Being rudely stripped of my shroud, I was placed naked on a table. In a short time I heard by the bustle in the room that doctors and students were assembling. When all was ready, the Demonstrator took his knife and pierced my bosom. I felt a dreadful cracking, as it were, throughout my whole frame; a convulsive shudder instantly followed, and a shriek of horror rose from all present. The ice of death was broken up; my trance was ended. The utmost exertions were made to restore me, and in the course of an hour I was in full possession of all my faculties."'

Surely John Macintire must have been the only person, other than the surgeons, ever to have welcomed the activities of the body snatchers!

CHAPTER FIVE

FINALE FOR THE BODY SNATCHERS

No-one will ever know just how many graves were desecrated, how many bodies were sold to the dedicated surgeons by the unscrupulous resurrectionists, but sooner or later the appalling practice had to stop. Admittedly petitions had occasionally been raised but to no avail. One, entitled *Use of the Dead to the Living*, written by Southwood Smith and printed in 1828, suggested that the bodies of those persons who died in all infirmaries and hospitals, *unclaimed by immediate relatives* (Smith's italics), be appropriated to the purpose of anatomy, as would those in workhouses, poorhouses, houses of correction, gaols and prison hulks. His proposal was substantiated by returns studied by the subsequent Committee for Anatomy, which revealed that in the workhouses of 127 parishes in London in 1827 no fewer than 3,103 people who died therein, were buried in paupers' graves at the parishes' expense, and of these, well over a thousand had no relative attend their funerals. Had these corpses been handed over instead to the surgery schools for dissection purposes, not only would the parishes have saved money, but the body snatchers would have lost their jobs.

Regarding his inclusion of those who died in poorhouses, Smith made the point that 'these persons are pensioners upon the public bounty; they owe the public a debt; they have been supported by the public during life; if therefore after death they can be made useful to the public; it is a prejudice, not a reason – it is an act of injustice, not the observance of a duty, which would prevent them from becoming so. Nor is any indignity either intended or offered to these persons.

William Burke (from a sketch taken in court)

They are appropriated to this service [of being taken away and dissected!] not because they are poor, but because they are friendless; because, that is, no persons survive them who take such an interest in their fate as to be rendered unhappy by this disposal of their remains. That is the best possible reason why they should be selected for this service.' Friendless old age pensioners beware!

Little, if any, notice was taken of this or other petitions at the time, the eventual and inevitable change ironically coming about, not because of the public's sudden awareness and subsequent feelings of revulsion at the thought of bodies being dragged out of graves but by 'ordinary' murders, the bodies of the victims then being sold for the purposes of dissection.

Whenever the term 'body snatcher' is mentioned, two names immediately spring to mind, those of Burke and Hare – yet they of all people were not body snatchers at all.

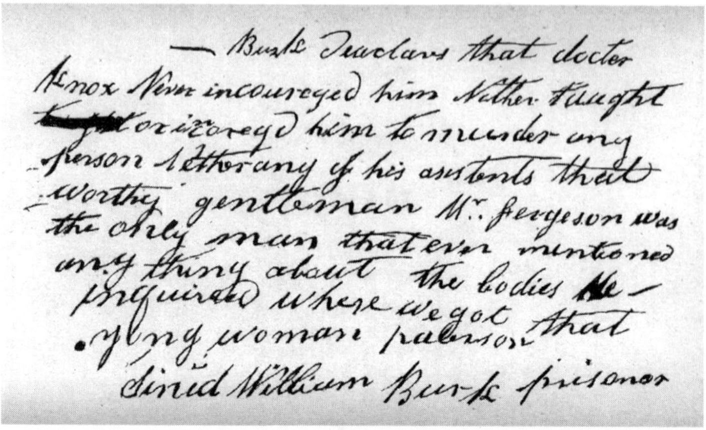
— Burke Declares that doctor Knox Never incouraged him Nather taught or incoraged him to murder any person Nether any of his asistants that worthy gentleman Mr. Fergeson was the only man that ever mentioned any thing about the bodies He inquired where we got that yong woman paterson
Sined William Burke prisoner

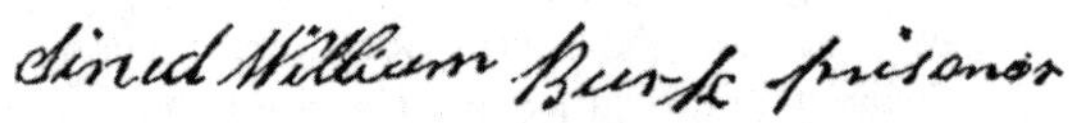

Part of Burke's confession and his signature

Nevertheless it was their criminal activities that brought the whole situation into the glare of publicity. Their story has been written extensively over the decades, but in outline, the account reported in the *Edinburgh Scotsman* of 28 January 1829 summed up their crimes.

'William Burke, lately a soldier in the Donegal Militia in which he was a fifer (played the flute), came out of Ireland and, after working for a time on the Union Canal in Scotland drifted into Edinburgh and took up his residence with a woman he had picked up in his travels, at the Beggar's Hotel, a headquarters for indigent Irishmen. He there started a small second-hand clothing business and also employed himself collecting and repairing discarded shoes, which his woman peddled around the town. In 1826 he moved to Log's boarding house in Tanner's Close and rented the basement apartment. This hostelry was run by William Hare, an ex-tenant, who had taken over the business, along with the widow of Log, the original proprietor.

On 29 November 1827 Burke was at work repairing a shoe in one of the rooms in the apartment when Hare came in and announced that one of his boarders, an old army pensioner

This sketch of Hare and his wife was made during the trial. The child was kept in court by its mother although it was suffering from whooping cough.

named Donald, had died, owing a board bill of amounting to £4. Donald left no property that could be seized for the bill and Hare suggested to Burke that he join him in selling the body to one of the medical schools. This was managed without any difficulties, the two men receiving £7.10 for the corpse. Shortly afterwards, one of Hare's boarders being taken ill with a fever, they were prepared to dispose of him in the same way. But he lingered on until Burke lost patience and hastened his end by placing a pillow over his face and smothering him. The body was then sold to the porter of Dr Knox's school.

Realising the ease with which they could enrich themselves at little risk, Burke and Hare began to befriend all the poor and vulnerable wretches they encountered. Their modus operandus involved finding a drunk on the streets, bringing him or her back home, then plying them with more drinks until they relapsed into a stupor. Burke would then sit on the victim's chest while Hare suffocated the victim by holding his hand over the mouth and nostrils, although Burke improved on this primitive method later by making a wax mask which was slapped on to the victim's face in order to bring about the necessary asphyxiation. In his later confession Burke described how when they kept the mouth and nose shut a very few minutes, they (the victims) could make no resistance but would convulse and make a rumbling noise in their bellies for some time; after they ceased crying and making a resistance they (the murderers) left them to die by themselves, but their bodies would often move afterwards, and for some time they would have long breathings before life went away'.

The business prospered and they had murdered and sold between twenty and thirty [actually the final total was believed to have been fifteen – author] before they made the mistake of disposing of an old beggar woman variously known as Mary Campbell, Margery M Gonigal, Duffie or Docherty. It happened that she had friends who saw her with Burke and when she disappeared from her usual haunts they went to the police and started an investigation. The body was found packed in a tea-box in the cellar of Dr Knox's house and the police learned from the porter that it had been delivered by Burke and Hare. They then searched Burke's house and found sufficient evidence of murder to hold the partners for trial. Hare testified for the State and escaped, but Burke was sentenced to death.

Being found guilty by a majority jury verdict of thirteen to two, sentence of death was passed on Burke decreeing that he was 'to be carried back to the Tollbooth of Edinburgh, therein to be detained and to be fed on bread and water only, until Wednesday 28 January next to come (1829) and upon that day to be taken forth to the common place of execution in the Lawnmarket of Edinburgh and then and there, between the hours of eight and ten o'clock before noon of the said day, to be hanged by the neck, by the hands of the common executioner, upon a gibbet, until he be dead, and his body thereafter to be delivered to Dr Alexander Monro, Professor of Anatomy in the University of Edinburgh, to be by him publicly dissected and anatomised' the Lord Justice-Clerk adding 'and I trust that if it is ever customary to preserve skeletons, yours will be preserved in order that posterity may keep it in remembrance of your atrocious crimes'.

A vast crowd of more than 20,000 spectators watched the execution, which took place in torrential rain, and as described by George MacGregor in his book *The History of Burke and Hare*, 'When the bolt was drawn by Williams, the hangman, the multitude set up a fearful yell, and every time the body of the dying man, a white cotton night-cap covering his head, gave a convulsive twitch, the crowd cheered to the echo. An eye witness said "He struggled a good deal and put out his legs as if to catch something (the edge of the drop) with his feet, but some of the undertaker's men, who were beneath the

The public execution of William Burke (from an etching by Walter Geikie,Edinburgh 1829)

drop, took him by the feet and sent him spinning round - a motion which continued until he was drawn up to the level of the platform". It was now fully a quarter past eight and Burke had been separated from this world'. After the body had been cut down and lowered into the coffin, spectators scrambled to snatch pieces of the rope, shavings from the coffin and strands of his hair as souvenirs.

The following day the corpse was taken to the anatomical theatre and placed on the black marble slab, where a sculptor, Mr Joseph, made a cast of it before operations began. During the dissection itself, rioting took place, doctors, students, business men, members of the public jostling and fighting to get a better view of the macabre performance. Gory it certainly

> was, a witness describing how, when the top of Burke's skull was removed 'the quantity of blood that gushed out was enormous, and by the time the lecture was finished, which was not until three o'clock, the area of the class-room had the appearance of a butcher's slaughter-house, from its flowing down and being trodden on'.
>
> On the following day no fewer than 25,000 members of the public queued up and were allowed to file past and inspect the remains on view, sixty a minute pausing momentarily to stare with morbid fascination at the dead murderer's face, now turning blue, the shaved head, with bloodstains not yet wiped off, the rictus smile, the wide-staring eyes, and it was recorded that 'at least seven females pressed in among the crowd which viewed the corpse, these women being roughly handled by some of the men present.'

In his book MacGregor quotes one who was present; 'After this exhibition Burke was cut up and put in pickle for the lecture-table. He was cut up into quarters, or rather portions, and salted and, with a strange aptness of poetical justice, put into barrels. At that time an acquaintance of mine was assistant to the professor and with him I frequently visited the dissecting room. He showed me Burke's remains and gave me the skin of his neck and of the right arm. These I had tanned, the neck brown, the arm white. The white was as pure as white kid but as thick as white sheepskin; the brown was like brown tanned sheepskin. It was curious that the mark of the rope remained on the leather after being tanned. Of the neck-leather I had a tobacco pouch made, and on the white leather of the arm I got Johnston to print the portraits of Burke and his wife, and Hare, which I gave to the noted antiquarian Mr Fraser, and it was in one of his cases for many years'. Macabre souvenirs indeed.

Following the trial Hare was escorted across the border into England for his own safety, the fact that he had given evidence against his partner proving totally unacceptable to the populace. It is believed that he found employment with a limeburner and, his identity being discovered by his fellow workers, he was blinded by being thrown into a vat of lime. He subsequently went to London and for about forty years afterwards became a blind beggar, his patch being the north side of Oxford Street.

Following the furore aroused in Scotland, concern spread throughout the country, dissecting rooms being torched and medical staff assaulted. Not that the London body snatchers appeared unduly concerned. In January 1829 the body of a man who had dropped dead on Walworth Common was brought to the workhouse and later claimed by a couple calling themselves Mr and Mrs Huntingdon, the latter averring that the dead man was her brother. Suspecting nothing, and only too relieved that the cost of a pauper's burial would not have to be met from parish funds, the authorities permitted the couple to take the body away after the inquest – which they did, direct to St Bart's Hospital, receiving with thanks the sum of eleven guineas!

However they were subsequently heard wrangling over the division of the spoils; the police were sent for and a search of their Southwark lodgings revealed not only the deceased's clothing, but also a full kit of body snatchers' tools – screw-drivers, gimlets of all sizes, even crowbar-like instruments used to wrench open coffin-lids. In court, however, they could only be charged with having stolen the dead man's clothes, and so received a merely nominal sentence.

Cases such as this continued to occur for some months until a bill to legalise the acquisition of bodies for dissection purposes passed through the House of Commons, one which would permit hospital and workhouse authorities to hand over any bodies unclaimed by relatives to authorised medical schools. However the House of Lords rejected the Bill on the not unreasonable grounds that it condemned the corpses of the poor to treatment which would not be meted out to corpses of the rich. Back to square one!

But the impasse was to be broken only a matter of months later. Enter John Bishop, a notorious resurrectionist who in twelve years of moonlighting, or rather, non-moonlighting, boasted of having dug up and sold between five hundred and a thousand bodies from London cemeteries. His business partner was Thomas Head who, after serving three years in prison, not only changed his name to Williams but his profession to the Burke and Hare method of acquiring bodies by murder and selling them.

The origin of their partnership was, to say the least, unusual. Bishop's father, a carrier plying between London and Highgate, had been married three times and after his death John, born of the first marriage, wasted no time in forming a conjugal relationship with his stepmother in order to be the recipient of her fifteen shillings a week pension. Although succeeding to his father's business, he soon sold it and, getting to know some body snatchers, became one himself.

One of his half-sisters was seventeen-year-old Rhoda and she happened to meet the man who lived next door to their house in Nova Scotia Gardens, just off the Hackney Road in Shoreditch, London. He was Thomas Head (who, changing his name, will be referred to henceforth as Williams). He had taken up residence there following his release from prison and such was their mutual attraction that they married. Thomas then moved in with his new wife and her half-brother John.

On their wedding night Rhoda beseeched Thomas not to get involved with body snatchers and on being questioned further, admitted that John had been a resurrection man for years. Rhoda's plea was as good as an invitation to a man with a criminal record; wasting no time, he joined Bishop as an accomplice, both already realising the potentialities of the now empty adjoining house. As a part-time job Williams also acted as porter to a firm of private glass blowers and in fact built up an illicit business of manufacturing glass himself. When No. 2 Nova Scotia Gardens was later raided by Excise officers, no less than 68 cwt of manufactured glass, 24 cwt of cullet and 16 cwt of iron, the two latter being ingredients used in the process, were discovered.

These two body snatchers, no doubt taking it for granted that they were far more clever than Burke and Hare and would not be caught in the same way, started befriending homeless men, women, even youngsters, bringing them back to their house – with the connivance of their wives – and plying them with gin and laudanum (a tincture of opium) until they collapsed in a stupor. A rope was then tied about the victim's ankles, who was then lowered head-first into a well in the garden. After any struggles had stopped and bubbles had ceased to rise, the body was left suspended for a while to 'allow the drugged liquor to drain from the body' as one of them later explained.

Returning to the well, the duo would hoist the drowned corpse to the surface and stripping it completely, dispose of the clothing via the privy in the empty house. After tying the body in the usual doubled-up position, it would be stowed in the waiting trunk, which was then securely roped in readiness for delivery by their porter, Shields, at that time living in Eagle Street, Red Lion Square. As the watchman and grave digger of the Roman Catholic Chapel, Moorfields, he was a valuable source of information.

This plan was put into action on several occasions, Shields carrying the large trunk on his head and, to allay suspicion, Mrs Rhoda Williams accompanied him carrying a hatbox. The two murderers walked on the opposite side of the road, keeping pace with them, near enough to ensure the safe delivery of the goods but far enough away to escape should the 'porter' be stopped and searched.

The system worked well, the corpses being sold for eight or ten guineas a time, leaving a nice profit for Thomas and John after Shields had received his ten shillings; needless to say, most of the money ended up in the till of the Flower Pot Inn in Bishopsgate or the Bell Tavern, Smithfield. But, inevitably, overconfidence was their downfall, this coming about when they offered their usual liquid hospitality to Carlo Ferrari, a young lad who scraped a living exhibiting white mice in the streets. After a few draughts of the deadly cocktail the lad collapsed and the murderers went out for a drink at the Feathers, near Shoreditch Church. On their return they attempted to lower him into the well but being only semi-conscious, the boy struggled, only being subdued after receiving several blows to the head.

Bishop, in his subsequent confession, recounted how 'we took him into the garden and tied a cord to his feet to enable us to pull him up by, and I then took him in my arms and let him slide from them headlong into the well, whilst Williams held the cord to prevent the body going altogether too low into the well. He was nearly wholly in the water in the well, his feet just above the surface. Williams fastened the other end of the cord around the paling, to prevent the body getting beyond our reach. The boy struggled a little with his arms and legs in the water; the water bubbled for a minute. We waited till these symptoms were past and then went down Shoreditch'. Three quarters of an hour later the two men returned, hauled up and trussed the body, placed it in the trunk, went to bed. The next morning they contacted another of their profession, a man called May, to ascertain which surgeon was paying the best prices.

James May was the illegitimate son of a barrister, his mother being the laundress in the building in which her lover had his office. James had a fairly good education and worked for a firm of solicitors at the age of fourteen but was dismissed for

John Head (alias Thomas Williams) and John Bishop (from drawings by WH Clift made directly after their execution

mixing with the unsavoury characters who congregated in Clare Market. He then became a butcher, a trade which he probably found useful later when handling the dead bodies he had exhumed. To facilitate easy access to his victims he took lodgings in a house in Clement's Lane which fortuitously happened to overlook the burial ground of St Clement Dane's workhouse in neighbouring Portugal Street, although of course he was never averse to digging elsewhere to make an easy guinea or more.

Having given Bishop and Williams the benefit of his opinion, he accompanied the other two villains in a hired cab and returned to the house to collect the young boy's body. On arrival May, by nature even more despicable than Bishop, promptly suggested that the teeth could be sold separately and, calling for a bradawl, proceeded to gouge a dozen of them out. Later, while having a drink in the Fortune of War Inn, a tavern much favoured by resurrection men, he passed the time by washing them in a glass of water, with negligible results, for when he sold them the next day to a dentist, Thomas Mills of 39 Bridge House Place, Newington Causeway, for the princely sum of twelve shillings, they still had pieces of flesh and jaw-bone adhering to them.

James May had recommended Guy's Hospital and Grainger's Anatomical Theatre but both of these institutions declined their offering, so the four of them, Shields having joined the party by now, went to King's College. On arrival they deposited the body on the floor for inspection by Mr Hill, the dissecting room porter. He immediately noticed the serious injuries and bloodshot eyes of the corpse. Further evidence of foul play became apparent to him when he saw that the left arm was bent and the fingers clenched, sure signs that the body had not been in a coffin, so he sent for Mr Partridge, the anatomical demonstrator, making sure he didn't alarm the waiting gang by telling them he needed his superior's approval. On seeing the state of the corpse Mr Partridge stalled them, making the excuse that he needed to get change for a fifty pound note, and then returned with the police. Having spent most of the day in various inns, all four were by then fighting drunk, especially May who had to be frog-marched to the police station 'with his smock-coat turned up over his head to stop him biting the constables'.

A search of the house revealed not only Carlo's white mice, with which Bishop's children were playing, but a cache of clothes and valuables belonging to their various victims, together with the blood-stained bradawl used by May. With such damning evidence the result was a foregone conclusion. On 5 December 1831 Bishop, Williams and May were charged at the Old Bailey with committing wilful murder and were found guilty, the packed public gallery being graced by the presence of the Duke of Sussex. Bishop and Williams were sentenced to be hanged and dissected but Shields, not having participated in the murder of Ferrari, was released without charge. May escaped the death penalty and when told this, he fell to the ground in a fit, the blood leaving his face and lips, his arms waving so convulsively that it took four of the prison officers to hold him down, and a quarter of an hour elapsed before he regained his full senses. He was however sentenced to be transported for life, but died on board the prison hulk *Grampus* in the following year.

By 2 am on the day of the executions two thousand people had already packed the area around Newgate Prison, and by daybreak this number had increased to more than thirty thousand. Seats in surrounding balconies were hired out, with prices starting at one guinea and rising to ten guineas depending on their proximity to the scaffold. *The Observer* newspaper commented that 'not only in the crowd were numbers of the fair sex, but the windows were chiefly filled with them. On the roofs of the houses persons of both sexes

William Calcraft the hangman at Bishops and Williams' execution. He kept the post of public hangman longer than any other man and was responsible for the last public hanging.

had placed themselves in situations of such danger as to excite a strong apprehension for their safety, many having no other safeguard than a hold of the chimney pots to prevent them from rolling down the sloping roofs. Two hundred special constables were sworn in by the Lord Mayor'. But despite all these precautions, the crowd was so vast that when the iron supports of a barrier at the end of Giltspur Street gave way, scores of men and women were crushed, those badly injured being taken to St Bart's Hospital.

The hangman was William Calcraft, an executioner whose past victims would, were they able, be reluctant to thank him for a pain-free launch into the unknown, for his practice of using a short rope (one of which, a mere three feet in length, can be seen on display in Lancaster Castle) brought agonising

Calcraft's notorious short drop rope preserved in Lancaster Castle

death by slow strangulation rather than by instant severing of the vertebrae. Yet his method was accepted without comment by the authorities of the day and was in fact welcomed by the vengeful public and those enthusiasts who wouldn't miss a public hanging for the world.

It is ironic that he of all people should have been instrumental in despatching members of a gang supplying dentists with teeth so callously removed from their dead victims, for Calcraft himself, while plying his pre-hangman trade of selling pies at hangings, became acquainted with hangmen James Foxen and Thomas Cheshire and, on being told of the lucrative demand for molars, had assisted his friends by extracting teeth from the jaws of those they had just executed!

As the London executioner, Calcraft had no qualms about dealing with Bishop and Williams in his own inimitable style; Bishop died fairly quickly but Williams struggled in the death throes for several minutes to the accompaniment of the cheers from the bloodthirsty mob packed around the scaffold, several of whom then proceeded to break through the barriers. Many were injured in the melee which followed, some being trampled underfoot, and by half past seven that morning between twenty and thirty of the rioters, seriously maimed, were conveyed to St Bart's Hospital.

The bodies were left hanging and not cut down until an hour had elapsed, as required by the law, and a witness described the scene that followed. 'A small cart drove up to the scaffold and the bodies were placed in it, covered with two sacks. The cart then moved on at a slow place, followed by the sheriffs, the city marshal and a large party of constables, along Giltspur Street to No. 33 Hosier Place, the house of Mr Stone the surgeon, the vast crowd lining the route yelling and making discordant noises as they proceeded. At the house it was with great difficulty that the bodies were removed from the cart, the crowd appearing more than anxious to gain possession of them themselves. The bodies were placed on a table and in the presence of the sheriffs, in conformity with their duty, an incision was made in their chests. The bodies were later removed, Bishop's to King's College (!) and Williams' to the Theatre of Anatomy in Windmill Street, Haymarket, to be dissected. They were publicly exhibited on Tuesday and Wednesday at both places, when immense crowds of persons were admitted to see their remains.'

This practice of displaying anatomical specimens continued well into the nineteenth century. For example *A Catalogue or Guide to the Liverpool Museum of Anatomy, 29 Paradise Street*, published in 1877, gives brief descriptions of upwards 'of 1000 models and diagrams procured at the anatomical galleries of Paris, Florence and Munich'. The exhibition included such fascinating items as 'a well-formed female pelvis; four skulls of newly-born babies; two sections of the human skull; the exterior view of two breasts, one that of a virgin, the other that of a mother; a Hungarian nobleman from whose head a horn protruded and he, in consequence, grew bald-headed; the daughter of the above who had a horn on her cheek and another on her forehead; the head and face of William Palmer, executed for murder; life-size models of two children who were born of syphilitic parents, with congenital chancres and sores over their whole bodies' and other similar stomach-churning subjects no doubt avidly studied by the general public on a wet Liverpudlian afternoon.

So great was the public outcry against the trade in corpses in general and Bishop, Williams and May in particular, that although the cheering, jeering crowds surrounding the scaffold that day could hardly have been aware of it, they were in effect applauding the virtual extinction of the body snatching fraternity. Scathing attacks on the need to exhume the bodies of the innocent dead appeared in the newspapers, one correspondent proposing instead that because prostitutes had by their bodies during life been engaged in corrupting mankind, it was only right that after death those bodies should be handed over to be dissected for the public good. Another writer cast his net more widely, advocating that the bodies of all suicides should be used for dissection, and that all those persons who 'came to their death by duelling, prize-fighting or drunken-ness should be handed over to the surgeons for a similar purpose'.

On 15 December 1831, just ten days after the double executions, the instigator of the original Bill, Member of Parliament Henry Warburton, seized the opportunity to submit a slightly amended version to the House of Commons, additional pressure being brought to bear on the government by the radical journalist and writer William Cobbett who, on 24 January following, published an emotional article in his paper *Twopenny Trash*.

> 'You have been informed of the horrible murders in London committed by the bloody Bishop and others, and I will now explain to you the cause of those murders. When you clearly see this cause, you will know how you ought to think and feel on the subject. There are in London and some other great towns, places where men are engaged in cutting up dead human bodies. What they do this for; that is to say, under what pretence they do this, I will speak by and by; at present I have only to speak of the fact, and to show you that it is the cause of the horrible murders that you have lately read of. The cutters-up of human bodies purchase dead bodies to cut up, and with just as little scruple and ceremony as cutting-butchers purchase the dead bodies of pigs or sheep from the carcass-butchers. The law

as it now stands makes it only a misdemeanour, that is to say, a crime punishable by a fine and imprisonment, as a common assault is, or as a libel is, to steal, to sell or to purchase a dead human body; and I pray you mark, that to steal the dead body of a sheep or pig or calf or ox or fowl or any sort, is a capital felony punished with death, and that to receive any such body, or to have it in your possession, knowing it to have been stolen, is also a felony, punishable with transportation.

But, my friends, if it be just, and it is so, to punish with transportation a man who received the dead body of a pig, knowing it to be stolen, what are we to say to the law that punishes so slightly and, in practice, punishes not at all, he who receives and cuts up the body of one of the people, though he must know that it has been stolen, if not murdered? What are we to say of such a law? And while the law stands thus, what is the protection that the labouring classes receive from the law?

Sixty poor persons, at the very least, have been murdered in London alone; probably hundreds, but sixty at least (the total then believed murdered by Bishop – author). And observe, they have all been received by the cutters-up, and no detection of the murderers ever took place until that of the bloody Bishop and his associates, whose conduct was so open and unwary that the receivers saw that they were likely to be implicated themselves in the crime of murder.

The College of Surgeons allow, that even they are not, in all cases, able to distinguish between murdered bodies and bodies stolen from the coffin. The cutters-up and the receiver never know that they are not accessories to the commission of murder, they proceed in their bloody work, knowing that they may be such accessories. No man, nothing short of a monster, will deny that it is as great a crime to steal the dead body of a human being as it is to steal the dead body of a sheep or a pig. Therefore, that crime ought to be punished with death as is the crime of stealing the dead body of a pig or sheep; and death ought to be the punishment of the receiver and the cutter-up'.

Not that Cobbett wasn't above doing a little body-snatching of his own, albeit it for purely altruistic reasons, of course. One of his closest friends was the Radical, Tom Paine (1737-1809), author of *The Rights of Man*, an ardent supporter of the French Revolution – he even became a Deputy in the French Revolutionary Government – and also of the American fight for independence. Ten years after Paine's death in America,

Cobbett decided that the 'Champion of Liberty' should not be left to lie in a country that did not appreciate him and so was determined to exhume his remains and bring them back to England where they would be honoured and commemorated. In his *Register* of September 1819 he admitted 'I have just done a thing I have always, since I came here (America) vowed I would do, that is, to take up the remains of Payne in order to convey them to England. In his old age and last days he was basely treated by his Republican rulers and by many besides. Even the Quakers refused him a grave.'

He continued: 'Our expedition set off from New York in the middle of the night, got to the place 22 miles off, called New Rochelle, and found Paine buried in the corner of a barren, rugged field. We took up the coffin entire, brought it off to New York, and just as we found it, it goes off to England'. He escorted the remains of his friend across the Atlantic in the ship *Hercules* and landed at Liverpool on Sunday 21 November 1819. On the Wednesday after, his heavy luggage lying in the Custom House was examined. 'These, gentlemen,' said Cobbett, when a large wooden box was opened, revealing a skull and a coffin plate, 'are the mortal remains of the immortal Tom Paine'. Cleared by Customs, the box was despatched to Cobbett's house in Bolt Court, Fleet Street, London. But his good intentions faded and over the next few years rumours abounded that Tom Paine's skull adorned the bookshelf of a clergyman; that some of the bones were once in the possession of the Rev Robert Ainslie, sometime Secretary of the London City Mission, but were lost when the family moved away.

In April 1924 a letter appeared in the *Daily Telegraph* written by a Brighton lady who stated: 'My grandmother's first husband, Mr Wilkinson, was a Customs House officer in Liverpool at the time William Cobbett brought Tom Paine's bones for burial in England. William Cobbett gave Mr Wilkinson Tom Paine's jawbone. My grandmother thought so much of it that she took it with her when she became the new wife of Richard Beverley, schoolmaster of Eglwysbach, North Wales. My mother used to play with it when a child; but after her marriage and on a visit to her old home, she thought it should have a decent burial, and she eventually buried it in an open grave in the village churchyard'.

A booklet entitled *Thomas Payne's Bones and Their Owners* published in 1909 gave what purported to be a detailed account of the bones' travels. The box containing them did arrive in Bolt Court in 1819, where they remained until January 1833, when Cobbett moved to Normandy Farm, Surrey. Cobbett died on 18 June 1835 and his son William carved Paine's name on different places of the skull and on certain bones for identification, pending the sale by auction of the farm and effects. The auctioneer would not accept the bones as being auctionable and in 1847 the box passed via the trustee Mr West to Benjamin Tilly, an old friend of Cobbett's, then lodging with a family called Ginn in Stepney.

Tilley, by then an old man, embarked in business but failed, and his goods were seized for debt, but at Richard's Auction Rooms in Rathbone Place, a London publisher Mr J Watson bought the box that few others knew contained Paine's bones. Yet oddly enough the remains were later reported as still being in Ginn's house at the time of Tilley's death, for on one occasion the bones were seen in a bag by Mr Ginn, and Mrs Ginn declared that she gave them to a ragman with rubbish she'd collected when clearing Tilly's room out. Perhaps the only person who knew was the Rev George Russell, an aged Baptist minister of Stepney at that time, who bought some of Cobbett's papers from the Ginns – for among them was reportedly a piece of Tom Paine's dried brain which Tilly had cut away. So should anyone come across a skull or bones inscribed T P ...? Curiously enough a skull alleged to be that of Tom Paine was auctioned in Australia in 1988 and bought by a man claiming to be descended from the long-deceased Paine but, like so many similar relics of saints and radicals, absolute proof being in short supply, its provenance remains doubtful.

But let us revert to 1831. When Henry Warburton re-submitted his Bill to the House of Commons, the Members acted with unwonted alacrity. Parliament passed it through the various stages, and it finally received the Royal Assent on 1 August 1832, the regal stroke of the pen bringing to an end once and for all the abhorrent practice of exhuming dead bodies and making at least two hundred body snatchers redundant with immediate effect.

Omitting the legal verbiage, the Anatomy Act decreed that; all surgeons and their equivalents, anatomists, professors, teachers etc. had to be licensed; the anatomical premises to be inspected regularly; the person having lawful possession of a body must permit it to undergo dissection unless the deceased had previously expressed a wish not to be so treated, either in writing and signed or expressed verbally, before two or more witnesses; or if a surviving spouse or relative insists on interment. It will be legal for those authorised, to dissect or anatomise bodies; after dissection, the body must be placed in a coffin or suitable shell and be given a decent burial in the appropriate cemetery. The Act which sentenced murderers to be dissected as part of their punishment was repealed (thereby removing the stigma from those innocent people whose bodies were dissected).

An interesting endorsement of this Act which, once and for all, meant that no more would churchyards be robbed of their silent tenants, was forthcoming when many of the highest in the land, among them the Duke of Sussex, the youngest son of King George III, and uncle of Queen Victoria, gave instructions that their bodies should be anatomised after death. Nevertheless, there were sections of society who, for some years, still refused to accept the now legally controlled schools of anatomy, as evidenced by the violent attack on one such, as reported by *Burgin's Sheffield Paper* of 9 January 1835 (with acknowledgements to Derby Local Studies Library).

The article was headed 'The New Dissecting House Dissected! Or, the Extraordinary affair in Eyre Street, Sheffield, which took place on Sunday Jan. 26th. 1835, with the discovery of several dead bodies with an attempt, it is reported, of two men to Burke a woman'. The text continued

> 'Yesterday, Sunday, a most mysterious affair occurred in Eyre-Street, Sheffield. A New Dissecting House having been established in a house situated at the above place, about noon yesterday, a loud and horrid cry of MURDER was heard, and a report circulated that they were attempting to "Burke" a Man *(i.e. to murder him and sell his body – author)*. A mob assembled and very shortly the door was forced open, and two men were taken into custody. A general rush now took place, and it was said that a woman had sustained great injury about the neck, and that the men were attempting to strangle her. Human bones were carried about in different directions; there was one body found and partly dissected, his bowels were *(had been?)* taken away, and some other parts were cut off; he had one of his stockings on. Crowds of people now assembled about the place, and had it not been for the timely and praiseworthy interference of the Police, the work of slaughter and destruction

would have been immense.

Nothing could exceed the fury of the mob,' the report continued, 'who cried out all of a mind, and they groaned most hideously; notwithstanding the house was strongly guarded by the Police and Watch of the Town; the windows of the house were assailed with stones, and the Landlord of the house shouted with a loud voice "Kill, Burn and Destroy him!"

About eight o'clock this morning, Monday, the scene of destruction commenced; the house was forced open by the exasperated mob, and every window of the house was, in a moment, dashed to pieces. The Furniture was hurled through the gutted windows, and beds, forms, chairs, &c. in frightful succession, were heaped together and set fire to by the infuriated mob. The street is one complete blaze, and the City of Moscow, when on fire, is a tool to this terrible conflagration. Human skeletons were hanging upon the lamp posts near to the premises. The Riot Act (a warning delivered by a magistrate ordering the crowd to disperse, under pain of arrest) has been read, and the fury of the mob is terrible beyond all comprehension.

The fragments of the Household Furniture, and the Tools used in dissecting human bodies, were now piled in one huge mass in the middle of the street, and the whole was set fire too, and are now consuming to ashes by the fiery element. The yells and shouting of the multitude is truly terrific. Different parts of human bodies have been exhibited in the neighbourhood of the house. An attempt was made to bring the Fire Engines to the place, but they could not succeed until Soldiers came to the assistance of the Engine Men'.

The two men were likely to have been innocent laboratory assistants, and the bodies, medical specimens; the 'injured woman' was obviously fictitious, not being mentioned again.

Let us end this chapter on a somewhat lighter tone. In a letter written by a Mr Boys to his doctor, Dr Campbell, written four years before his death in 1835 (i.e. written prior to the Act), he suggests a more agreeable, indeed fragrant method of disposing of his remains, viz. 'Are you now disposed to accomplish my wish, when my breath or spirit shall have ceased to animate my carcase, to perform the operation of vitrifying my bones (turning them into glass) and sublimating (purifying) the rest, thereby cheating the Devil of his due, according to the ideas of some devotees among Christians? And that I may not offend the olfactory nerves of my female friends with a mass of putridity, if it be possible, let me fill a few little bottles of essential salts therefrom, and revive their drooping spirits. It may be irksome to you to superintend the business but perhaps you have knowledge of some rising genius or geniuses who may be glad of a subject without paying for it. Let them slash and cut and divide, as best please 'em!'

In other words, he requested that his bones be converted into glass phials, his flesh etc. refined and added to appropriate minerals; then, having been thus converted into bottles of smelling salts, presented to his girlfriends! Alas we shall never know whether Dr Campbell obeyed his instructions, and if so, what effect the inhalation of his powdered and diluted remains had on the drooping spirits of his female admirers – ugh!

CHAPTER SIX

BODY SNATCHING ABROAD

Much to this country's discredit, there was no body snatching – or comparatively little – in Europe. So how did their surgeons teach anatomy? Without much difficulty, for they had few problems in obtaining specimens. For instance, following the 18th-century French Revolution, the law stipulated that the bodies of all those who died in hospital and prisons and were unclaimed within twenty-four hours of their death were to be made available for dissection, usually being transferred to the medical schools after dark. Other details obtained from the head of anatomy in Paris were published in *The Use of the Dead to the Living* previously mentioned, these briefly being; 'that a gratuity of eightpence is given to the attendants in the hospitals for each body; that the chief of the anatomical department of the faculty of Paris sends a carriage daily to the different hospitals to bring back the necessary number of bodies, this number totalling between 1,000 to 2,000 per year; that the price of bodies varies from four shillings to eight shillings and sixpence; that other anatomical departments have opened in all the great hospitals. Also, that after dissection the bodies are wrapped in cloths and carried to a neighbouring cemetery, where they are received for tenpence and that the practice of exhumation is abolished, orders for exhumation only being granted for legal reasons'.

The head of the department also pointed out that the public understands the need for dissection and the relatives of the deceased seldom or never oppose the opening of any body, if the physicians require it. Obviously then there was an adequate supply of bodies, eliminating the need for body snatchers, and in the unlikely event of a criminal being tempted, the penalty for violating a place of sepulchre was sufficient to deter him – imprisonment for three to twelve months and a maximum fine of 200 francs.

One major exhumation and re-interment with far more humane intent occurred during and after the Revolution. After he was guillotined, Louis XVI's corpse was placed in a long wicker basket and taken by the executioner Sanson's cart to the Madeleine Cemetery where a trench six feet wide and ten feet deep had already been dug. The corpse, its head laid between its legs, the face not discoloured, and the eyes wide open, was not taken into church, but placed in a pinewood coffin, and after a brief absolution, was carried to the grave side. Quicklime was poured over the remains, the coffin lowered into the grave, and the earth filled in.

Following the later execution of his Queen, Marie Antoinette, her coffin was deposited near to his, and the exact location was noted by a M. Desclozeaux and his son-in-law, who, in 1795, purchased the graveyard with the pious object of commemorating the spot and there they planted weeping willows. The remains lay undisturbed for more than twenty years, when M. Desclozeaux informed King Louis XVIII, and on 18th and 19th January 1815 excavations took place when the remains of the King and Queen, together with shreds of their clothing (even the Queen's garters), were transferred to lead coffins and sealed with the royal crest. On 21 January 1815, the twenty-second anniversary of the King's execution, the sad procession took the same route as that taken by him on his journey to the guillotine. Through streets lined with silent crowds, hearses conveyed the coffins to St Denis where they were laid to rest in the Bourbon vaults. Back in the cemetery, the Chapelle Expiatoire was built 'in expiation of the crime by which they had died'. Within it were erected marble statues of the King and Queen, with inscriptions in gold around their bases. In the crypt, over the exact spot where the royal couple had been buried so ignominiously, a marble sarcophagus was placed containing some of the earth and quicklime found adhering to their bones. Truly, the Desclozeaux were 'body snatchers' of the highest imaginable principles.

In Germany the bodies of suicides and those who died in prison were given to medical schools unless their relatives or friends were prepared to pay a certain amount of money to the medical schools in lieu. In other words they bought the body from the surgeon, in marked contrast to the English body snatching system. Because other sources of supply were available, such as the corpses of those who had died in the poorhouse, those who had left insufficient funds for their burial, and those considered outcasts of society such as men and women executed for their crimes, including 'public women' (prostitutes), resurrection men were unknown. Similarly in Austria, where the bodies of hospital patients unclaimed after forty-eight hours were given to the surgeons, the supply of corpses from the General Hospital was more than adequate for the medical schools in the capital, Vienna.

In Italy body snatching was unheard of, the corpses of those dying in hospital being made available. They could be handed over to relatives on payment of the funeral expenses, although reportedly this latter arrangement rarely occurred. The poorhouses too were always a bountiful source, thereby avoiding burial at public expense. After the requisite funeral service the bodies were temporarily stored in the local parish church until nightfall, each place of worship having a chamber assigned specifically for that purpose, and the corpses were then delivered to the dissecting rooms. Portugal followed the same system, especially where babies were concerned, as their infant mortality rate was particularly high.

The Dutch surgeons of the Dissecting School of Leyden never ran short of specimens as the civil hospitals in Amsterdam provided them with an adequate sufficiency. Lectures of anatomy were given to the public in all the principal towns, during which dissected subjects were exhibited.

Conditions in the United States of America were, however, somewhat different. The laws of the various states varied. Massachusetts, for instance, in 1784 went part way to solving the problem by enacting a statute declaring that 'When it shall appear by the coroner's inquest that any person had been killed in fighting in a duel, the coroner of the county where the act was committed, shall be, and he hereby is directed and empowered to take effectual care that the body of such person so killed be immediately secured and buried without a coffin with a stake drove through the body at or near the usual place of execution – or shall deliver the body to any surgeon or surgeons, to be dissected and anatomized, that shall request the same and engage to apply the body to that use.' This method of disposal also applied to the 'winner' of the duel after that person's trial and execution.

In many of the states there was plenty of scope for the resurrection men to operate, especially some of those in the south, their task being made even easier by the fact that many bodies were buried without first being enclosed in coffins. The two great medical schools of the day were situated in Philadelphia and Baltimore. Body snatchers found ready markets there, providing cadavers exhumed from the local 'Potter's Fields', the burial places of the poorer classes, and because the authorities accepted the need for medical learning but were as reluctant to take action to legalise any acceptable alternative as were those in this country, the body snatchers flourished. Many surgeons got blamed, the public believing them to be personally involved in exhuming dead bodies. One particularly violent instance occurring on Sunday 13 April 1788, as graphically described in *Thacher's American Medical Biography* written in 1828.

> 'The outbreak around the New York Hospital was in consequence of a suspicion that the physicians of the city had robbed the graveyards to procure subjects for dissection. The concourse assembled on this occasion was immense and, some of the mob having forced their way into the dissecting-room, several human bodies were found in various states of mutilation. Enraged at this discovery, they seized upon the fragments such as heads, legs and arms, and exposed them from the windows and doors to public view, with horrid imprecations. The rioters had now become so outrageous that both the civil and military authorities were summoned to quell the tumult, and the medical students were confined in the common prison for security against the wild passions of the populace.'

Nor was this the end of the affair, for twelve days later the *Pennsylvania Journal and Weekly Register* described the following events.

> 'On the Monday (14 April) a number of people collected and were determined to search the houses of the suspected physicians. His Excellency the Governor, His Honor the Chancellor and His Worship the Mayor, finding that the passions of the people were irritated, went among them and endeavoured to dissuade them from committing unnecessary

depredations. They addressed the people pathetically and promised them every satisfaction which the laws of the country can give. This had a considerable effect upon many who, after examining the houses of the suspected doctors, returned to their homes.

But in the afternoon the affair assumed a different aspect. A mob, more fond of riot and confusion than a reliance upon the promises of magistrates and obedience to the laws, went to the gaol and demanded the doctors who were there be imprisoned. The Magistrates, finding that the mild language of persuasion was of no avail, were obliged to order out the militia to suppress the riot, to maintain the dignity of government, and to protect the gaol. A small party of about eighteen armed men assembled at three o'clock and marched thither, the mob permitting them to pass through, with no other insult than a few volleys of stones, dirt, etc. Another party of about twelve men, about an hour later, made a similar attempt but, having no orders to resist, the mob surrounded them and destroyed their arms. This gave the mobility fresh courage; they then endeavoured to force the gaol but were repulsed by a handful of men who bravely sustained an attack of several hours. They then destroyed the windows of that building with stones and tore down part of the fence. At dusk another party of armed civilians marched to the relief of the gaol and as they approached it, the mob, huzzaing, began a heavy fire with stones, brickbats, etc.'

Such was the intensity of the attack that it was reported:

'The Governor declared his intention to resort to the most vigorous and decisive measures for quelling the riot. General Baron von Steuben, in the benevolence of his heart, remonstrated with the Governor against ordering the militia to fire, when, in the midst of his harangue, he was struck in the forehead by a brickbat which, according to the Governor's account, not only knocked the good Baron down, but overset his humanity and brought his compassion, with his body, to the ground, which he no sooner touched than he cried out lustily "Fire, Governor, fire!"' The militia, doubtless only too willing to obey the order in their own defence, did so, three or four persons being killed and a number wounded, these casualties forcing the mob to disperse. On the Tuesday morning militia commanded by General Malcolm, together with Colonel Bauman's Regiment of Artillery, arrived and, with a detachment from each under arms at the scene, order was restored. By a macabre coincidence two men, George Swinney and Isaac Gano were arrested and charged on the same day as the riots, with having entered the cemetery of the Protestant Episcopal Church in Manhattan and a dead body of a certain white woman then lately buried there, did then and there dig up and take out of the same Coffin, and carry away, to the evil example of others in like cases offending against the Peace of the People of the State of New York and their Dignity.'

The logical assumption would be that these two felons were responsible for purveying the other corpses to those doctors whose houses had been attacked by the mob.

The public outcry which followed these outrages resulted in an Act being passed in 1789 'to prevent the odious practice of digging up and removing, for the purpose of dissection, dead Bodies interred in cemeteries or burial places', the penalties for those caught was to stand in the pillory or be whipped, fined and/or imprisoned as the courts might direct. The Act also provided for the corpses of murderers, arsonists and burglars to be handed over for dissection and, doubtless with the riots in mind, a Statute in the following year made it a crime punishable by a fine not exceeding 100 dollars and imprisonment not exceeding twelve months, to attempt to rescue a corpse from the house of any surgeon involved. But as the number of available cadavers of murderers, arsonists and burglars was obviously inadequate, body snatching continued undeterred. Cases were reported from Baltimore in 1807, Zanesville in 1811, St Louis in 1844, Illinois in 1848 and Cincinnati in 1852.

One was reported in detail in the *New York Evening Post* of 20 May 1824 which described how:

'At the late Court of Sessions, Solomon Parmeli was indicted for a misdemeanour, in entering Potter's Field and removing the covers of two coffins deposited in a pit and covered partly with earth. The statute making it a felony to dig up or remove a dead human body with intent to dissect it did not embrace this case because the prisoner had not dug up or removed the body.

Mr Shureman, the present keeper of Potter's Field, suspected that some person had entered it for the purpose of removing the dead and after sending for two watchmen and calling his faithful dog, he went to ascertain the fact. On arriving at the grave he found his suspicion confirmed, and requested

> the person concealed in the pit to come out and show himself. No answer being given, Mr Shureman sent his dog into the pit and in the twinkling of an eye, a tall stout fellow made his appearance and took off across the field. The night being dark, he might have effected his escape had it not been for the sagacity and courage of the dog, who pursued him for some distance, but at last came up with him, seized and held him fast until the arrival of the keeper and the watchmen, who secured him. The jury convicted the prisoner and the Court sentenced him to six months imprisonment in the Penitentiary.'

The name 'Potter's Field' was frequently applied to burial grounds in England and the USA, this being a generic term for sites in which unidentified corpses and those who were bereft of relatives were interred. The name is taken from the Bible (*Matthew xxvii*) and refers to the occasion on which 'the high priests purchased a field with the thirty pieces of silver returned to them by the conscience-stricken Judas, and they took counsel, and bought with them the potter's field, to bury strangers in.'

In Hartford, Connecticut, it was reported that on 17 May 1824:

> 'Two young ladies were taking a walk in the South burial ground when they discovered a tape-string and a piece of cloth which, upon examination, was found to be the piece that was laced upon Miss Jane Benton's face, who came to her death by drowning, and was buried a few days since. The ladies then went to the grave and found that it had been disturbed; that she had been taken out of her coffin by means of a rope around her neck. These circumstances have produced great excitement in the public mind and everyone is on the alert to discover the perpetrators of this unfeeling and brutal act. The citizens turned out in a body (!) yesterday and interred the corpse again.'

As in earlier years, such incidents provoked mob violence and this one was no exception. The corpse having been located in the Yale Medical College, that building was stormed but, as it was defended by armed students and the militia, the attackers were beaten back with no serious injuries being reported.

A traumatic instance involving the recognition of a corpse occurred when Mr John Scott Harrison, who had been an honoured member of the United States Senate and was the son of the ninth President of the United States, died on 26 May

1878. He was buried three days later in the cemetery at North Bend, Ohio. A few days later his son, Benjamin Harrison, who was elected President in 1888, went to the Ohio Medical College. in Cincinnati to look for the remains of a friend (for what reason was not stated) His shock and horror can only be imagined, when he also found the body of his father! A later report averred that the officials of the College were not responsible for this act but, assuming this to be true, the corpse could only have been obtained from body snatchers.

CHAPTER SEVEN

BODY PARTS AS SOUVENIRS

The body parts of some corpses, such as those of kings and queens, national leaders, aristocrats and notorious criminals, were acquired by grave robbers, albeit of a different calibre. They were not to be dissected but to be worshipped in holy places, exhibited in public, or gloated over in private as prized souvenirs.

The cadavers of kings and queens in particular were always a target for vandals; to put it crudely, everyone wanted a bit of a royal! The fact that one regal corpse had been deprived of its jawbone, hit the headlines on 28 April 1916 when the *Star* reported that:

> 'Expert visitors to the Royal Tombs at Westminster Abbey all know that many portions of the tombs have been stolen, but it will be news to many that the skeleton of Richard II was for over ninety years minus its jawbone. Thanks to a clergyman, the jawbone was returned. The loss was kept secret for many years, but it has now got out, and a *Star* man is now able to give all the facts about the matter, as disclosed by an Abbey verger.
>
> The story commences about a hundred years ago when the boys attending Westminster School used the Abbey as a sort of playground. They were allowed to wander at will, and one small boy, more curious than the rest, discovered in the tomb of Richard II, then in a very decayed condition, a hole large enough to put his hand in. The boy fished about in the hole and brought out what later proved to be the jawbone of the late King. He took his find to the school playground and the jawbone was examined with great interest until the arrival of a monitor (a senior boy) who, it is related, boxed the boy's

ears. The monitor, however, instead of returning the jawbone to its rightful owner, took it home. His father, interested in the discovery and having verified the fact that it was the tomb of Richard II which had been raided, placed the jawbone on a plush mount under a glass case and carefully labelled it "JAWBONE OF RICHARD II". And the relic was subsequently handed down to his family and successors.

Meanwhile the tomb itself was becoming more and more decayed, and later in the century it was renovated. The bones of the King were carefully removed and replaced, and it was when the renovation was complete that it was first noticed that the jawbone was missing.

In the reign of Edward VII (1901-1910) the jawbone came into the possession of a clergyman. Whether he was a descendant of the school monitor is not clear, but his conscience was not easy about the matter and he wrote to King Edward about it. His Majesty took an interest in the matter, and the authorities, having satisfied themselves beyond reasonable doubt that the jawbone was that of Richard II, decided that it should be returned to the tomb.'

Not a jawbone but hair from the head of Henry IV (1367-1413) was 'acquired' by Francis Trevelyan Buckland (1826-1888), an eccentric Victorian who at one time was assistant surgeon to the 2nd Life Guards. Whether this relic was acquired from the royal tomb or had been passed down through the ages from a 14th-century Court barber is not known, but Buckland added it to his collection of rarities which also included fragments of a Siberian dinosaur. He was an ardent naturalist and additionally believed that most creatures, even insects, were edible, demonstrating it by eating such unappetising dishes as flies, slugs, even broiled elephant's trunk. But perhaps his epicurean *piece de resistance* occurred when, while dining with an acquaintance, he is reported to have announced that although he had had many a strange repast in his time, never before had he eaten a king's heart – and he then proceeded to consume the heart of Louis XIV which, doubtless cooked, lay on his plate! If true, the desecration could probably have taken place when many of the royal tombs were vandalised during the French Revolution.

Although purloining internal organs for cannibalistic purposes was a distinct exception, any body part was considered to be a worthwhile, sometimes even a useful, souvenir. After the execution in Whitehall of Charles I, his body was displayed to the public in St James' Palace and then taken to Windsor Castle for burial in St George's Chapel there. Within the chosen vault were found two other coffins, one large one containing, as had been surmised, the remains of King Henry VIII with shreds of a purple pall still attached to its lid. The other, a smaller one, was that of Jane Seymour, Henry's third wife. While workmen were engaged in cutting 'King Charles, 1648' (the Julian calendar was then still in force) in a lead tablet to be secured to the coffin, the sexton reported that 'he had caught a foot-soldier in the chapel who had cut so much of Henry VIII's velvet pall as he judged would hardly be missed, and wimbled a hole in the coffin, probably fancying that there was something there well worth his adventure.' He (the sexton) said 'he had detained the sacrilegious person and on searching him, a bone from the royal coffin was found on him which, he admitted, he would have made into a knife haft.' The lead tablet having been attached to the lid, Charles I's coffin was then placed next to the other two coffins and the vault once more sealed up.

A hundred and sixty-five years later, in 1813, the vault was again opened and entered. The Prince Regent was present, as were the Duke of Cumberland, Count Munster, the Dean of Windsor and Sir Henry Halford, physician to the King, George III. A square opening was cut in the upper part of the lead coffin, of sufficient dimensions to enable the visitors to see that inside was a wooden coffin, very much decayed, and the body, wrapped in cere-cloth. This was removed above the face. The corpse was immediately recognised as that of Charles I, Sir Henry later reporting that 'When the head had been entirely disengaged from the attachments which confined it, it was found to be loose, and without any difficulty was taken up and held to view. The hair was thick at the back of the head and in appearance nearly black. A portion of it, which has since been cleaned and dried, is of a beautiful dark brown colour. That of the beard is of a redder brown. On the back of the head it was more than an inch in length, and had probably been cut so short for the convenience of the executioner.'

> On holding up the head to examine the place of separation from the body, the muscles of the neck had evidently retracted themselves considerably; and the fourth cervical vertebra was found to be cut through its substance transversely, leaving the surfaces of the divided portions perfectly smooth and even,

> an appearance which could have been produced only by a heavy blow, inflicted with a very sharp instrument, and which furnished the last proof wanted to identify King Charles I.'

Sir Henry Halford did not include everything in his report, for the accuracy of which the Prince Regent afterwards vouched. He omitted all mention of a truly deplorable scene. Before the King's burial in 1649, Mr Trapham, a London surgeon, had performed the usual practice of sewing the severed head to the trunk, and now the two parts had had to be separated before the head could be lifted out of the coffin. Some stitches had to be cut, others came away. And on lifting the head, the assistant, in the uncontrollable excitement of the moment, dropped the head on the stone floor, whereupon the Prince Regent swore at him and stalked out of the chapel.

Relieved of the royal presence, the rest of the party seem to have lost all sense of decency. Behaving like ghouls, they proceeded to help themselves to souvenirs, robbing the corpse of hair and chips of bone, one of the visitors even stealing one of Henry VIII's teeth from the adjacent, badly decayed coffin. The Royal physician himself cut off a lock of Charles' hair and later presented part of it, set in a gold locket, to the novelist Sir Walter Scott. Incidentally, a few strands of the King's hair recently re-emerged into the light of day, when auctioned in April 1995 for the sum of £3,910 to an American gentleman whose collection of hirsute appendages included a lock of Napoleon's hair (£345) and some strands of Henry IV's beard (£1,265).

Sir Henry Halford, not content with just the lock of hair, also removed and kept the King's fourth cervical vertebra. There are at least two conflicting accounts of what subsequently happened to it; one version alleges that Sir Henry used it as a salt cellar on his dining table for nearly thirty years (no doubt providing a fascinating topic of conversation among his dinner guests) until word of the desecration reached Queen Victoria. She, far from being amused, ordered it to be returned and so it was replaced in the tomb in a small casket.

The other, perhaps more credible account, is that the bone was passed down through Sir Henry's descendants until it came into the possession of the physician's grandson, also named Sir Henry Halford. He thought that this relic of a King should be returned to the royal family, and so he presented it to the Prince of Wales (later King Edward VII), who kept it, enclosed in a small ebony casket, on his private writing desk in Windsor Castle. However, a close personal friend took such a great dislike to it, and was obviously privileged sufficiently to express his or her distaste, that the Prince agreed to have the vertebra returned to the tomb.

This was carried out on 18 December 1888 at dusk, after a service in St George's Chapel. A sufficiently large aperture was made through the floor and brick archway of the vault. Escorted by the Dean and two Canons of Windsor, the Prince of Wales carried in the bone in its ebony box. Handkerchiefs were knotted together to form an improvised rope and the Prince knelt on the floor, slowly lowering the casket until at last it lay on but not in the coffin which contained the mortal remains of the King who had been so cruelly executed and frequently desecrated.

The corpses of queens, of course, were not immune to souvenir hunters either, and that of Catherine, consort of Henry V, was violated not so much by losing a bone or a lock of hair as by being deprived of a proper burial althogether, thereby having to submit to being touched at will by commoners. She had died in 1437, and her remains were placed in the Lady Chapel of Westminster Abbey.

Later the coffin was partially wrapped in a sheet of lead taken from the roof and, the lid not having been replaced, her body lay exposed from the waist up, it then becoming one of the 'attractions' of the Abbey to see and touch her desiccated corpse.

Described by the historian Dart as 'continuing to be seen, the bones being firmly united and thinly clothed with flesh, like scrapings of fine leather' it remained like that for many generations and was visited by Samuel Pepys, who wrote in his *Diary* that 'on Shrove Tuesday 1669 I to the Abbey went, and by favour did see the body of Queen Katherine of Valois, and had the upper part of the body in my hands, and I did kiss her mouth, reflecting on it that I did kiss a Queen; and this my birthday and I thirty-six years old and I did kiss a Queen.' A boastful comment bordering on necrophilia, the cadaver being two hundred and thirty-two years old. It was not until 1776 that decency eventually prevailed and Queen Catherine was reverently buried in the vaults.

There was no doubt about the sacrilege committed upon

the person of Queen Catherine, but controversy surrounds the remains of King James IV of Scotland, killed at the Battle of Flodden Field in 1513. The historian Stowe reported that after the battle the body was wrapped in lead and taken to the monastery at Sheen in Surrey. After the dissolution of the monasteries, the house in which the corpse was kept was acquired by the Duke of Suffolk. Stowe himself was shown the body 'still wrapped in lead, in a waste room among old timber and other rubble. Since the which time, workmen there, for their foolish pleasure, hacked off the head. And Launcelot Young, the master glazier, took the relic, it dry and retaining the red hair of its head and beard, but later caused the sexton of Wood Street Church to bury it.'

However, others say 'that the corpse was taken from the battlefield first to Berwick, thence to York and later to Richmond, where it was delivered to the King (Henry VIII) at the Charterhouse where it was to abide during the King's pleasure.'

Following the decapitation of Lady Jane Grey in the Tower of London, her head was buried with her body in the Royal Chapel of St Peter ad Vincula within that royal palace, but the head of her father, Henry Grey, Duke of Suffolk, was exhibited to the public for many years. After his execution as a 'traitor' (he had sought to overthrow Mary so that his daughter could remain sovereign), his head was retrieved from his coffin, probably by his widow and, because the family then had a mansion close to the Tower in what is now a street called the Minories, it was buried in a vault near the altar of their private chapel.

As the centuries passed, much rebuilding took place in the area, the Grey's chapel and house eventually being demolished and replaced by the Church of the Holy Trinity. And in 1851 the head was discovered in a small vault on the south side of the church altar. It was still thickly encrusted with oak sawdust from the scaffold basket into which it had fallen, the tannin in the oak having preserved it.

It was examined by Sir George Scharf, Keeper of the National Portrait Gallery who stated that its features corresponded to those in contemporary portraits, and a medical authority, Doctor Mouat, assessed it 'as belonging to a man past the prime of life, and that the head was removed by rapid decapitation during life admits of no doubt. A large gaping gash, which had not divided the subcutaneous structures, shows that the first stroke of the axe was misdirected, too near the occiput and in a slanting direction. The retraction of the skin, the violent convulsive action of the muscles, and the formation of a cup-like cavity in the body of the spinal bone at the base, prove that the severance was effected during life and in cold weather.'

The Church was closed down in 1899 and Henry Grey's head was transferred to St Botolph's Church, Aldgate. There, earlier in the twentieth century, it was possible, by courtesy of the vicar, to view the head in its airtight glass container. It was described by Sir George Younghusband in his book *The Tower of London*: 'There is no shrinkage of the face, the eyes are wide open and the eyeballs and pupils perfectly preserved. The skin too, all over, is of the same yellowish hue. When first found, the hair of the head and beard were still on, but owing to its very brittle state and from being handled by several people, these broke off, though in a strong light the bristles may still be seen. The nose is not quite perfect but the ears are practically as in life. The head had evidently been severed by two heavy blows, and loose skin, jagged and looking like loose parchment, demonstrates where the severance occurred.'

While living in the Tower of London as a yeoman warder in the 1970s, the author, with historic (or ghoulish!) curiosity, visited the church, only to be informed by the verger that the gruesome relic had been reverently interred some years earlier, beneath the paving stones at the church's entrance. Henry Grey's head had finally been laid to rest in consecrated ground, a mere arrow-flight from his daughter's grave within the Tower of London.

A much maligned sovereign, King John, who died stricken by dysentery at Newark in 1216 caused, according to a monkish chronicler, by a surfeit of peaches, wine and fresh cider, was buried in Worcester Cathedral. His body, clad in a monk's cowl as a disguise, was placed between the graves of two Saxon saints, Wulfstan and Oswald. In that way he hoped to hide from the divine retribution which he feared would be his fate after death. Worse however was to follow, for when the Cathedral was being renovated in July 1797, the public gained access to the tomb and it was reported that not only was one of the King's finger-bones stolen and, encased in silver, kept as a memento, but another obnoxious character is said to have abstracted a piece of decomposed flesh, baited his fish-hook with it and, having caught a fish, proceeded to run through the streets exulting over his macabre deed.

Not unlike the felons Roach, Elliot and Parker, mentioned in an earlier chapter who stole, not the corpse but its container, some despicable characters, as reported by the chronicler Stowe, retrieved the remains of King Stephen (1135-1154) from their resting place in Faversham Abbey, Kent, threw them into the river, and sold the lead coffin which had housed them.

There is seemingly no end to the sacrilegious vandalism inflicted on the corpses of national leaders. One notorious case was that of Oliver Cromwell. The Great Protector, suffering from the painful malady of gallstones, died on 2 September 1658. At the ceremony of lying-in-state in Somerset House, a magnificently robed wax image of him was positioned on a richly adorned bed and later, in the state funeral procession, the effigy, still clad in its royal robes, crowned and sceptred, was taken to Westminster Abbey in a special hearse drawn by six horses in trappings of black velvet. There it was displayed clad in a shirt of finest Holland, laced, doublet and breeches in Spanish fashion, silk stockings and black Spanish leather shoes, with a surcoat of purple velvet richly laced with gold lace, and wearing the royal crown.

His actual corpse had been buried earlier in a majestic tomb in the Abbey's Henry VII Chapel, because the embalming process had gone badly awry. Although the body had been filled with aromatic herbs and placed within a lead coffin, which in turn was enclosed in a wooden one, Cromwell's physician George Bate wrote 'The filth broke through them all, and it was prudent to bury him immediately, which was done in as private a manner as possible.' However, it was left in peace for only a little while longer than was its effigy. When Charles II ultimately resumed his rightful place on the throne, retribution against the Roundheads followed, particularly against those who had been instrumental in Charles I being condemned to death. And, dead or not, Cromwell had to pay the price. Parliament stated that 'Executions did not leave traitors in their graves, but followed them beyond it'.

On 30 January 1661 (ironically the twelfth anniversary of Charles I's execution) Cromwell's cadaver was roughly exhumed from its tomb by John Lewis, a mason, and an inscribed, double-gilded coffin plate found on the breast of the corpse was kept by the sergeant in charge of the guard.

The Triple Tree at Tyburn

The plate was later passed on by his daughter, Mrs Gifford, to a family named Hobart, and during the 19th century the unique artefact came into the possession of the then Marquis of Ripon.

The grim events which followed the exhumation were described by Sir George Wharton who in 1662 wrote: 'The odious carcases of O. Cromwell, H. Ireton and J. Bradshaw were drawn on sledges to Tyburn on the anniversary of the execution of Charles I and, being pulled out of their coffins, there hanged at the several angles of the Triple Tree till Sunset. Then taken down, beheaded, and their loathsome Truncks thrown into a deep hole beneath the Gallows. Their heads were afterwards set upon Poles on the top of Westminster Hall'.

Cromwell's coffin was not taken directly to Tyburn but took a more circuitous route via the Red Lion tavern, an inn which at that time stood at the south-west corner of the Square of the same name in Holborn where, guarded by soldiers, it remained overnight. Early the following morning the macabre cortege proceeded to Tyburn and the ghastly performance took place. A new gallows had been erected and Cromwell's corpse, wrapped in a green shroud, was 'hanged by the neck until the going down of the sun', when it was cut down and beheaded. The London hangman at that time was Edward Dun, an executioner not noted for his expertise, eight blows with the axe being required to sever the head from the already inanimate body.

As decreed by Parliament the torso was then buried beneath the gallows, and it may be significant that in *The Times* of 9 May 1860 it was reported that during excavations at the Tyburn site, workmen uncovered a quantity of bones. Since the remains of others who had been hanged there were almost invariably taken away for dissection or to display on the City's gates, the bones uncovered might well have been those of Cromwell and his two henchmen.

Some however disputed that Cromwell had been hanged at all. Despite the brandishing of the head after decapitation, its familiar features being visible to the crowds, rumours became rife that another corpse had been substituted during the overnight stay at the Red Lion. Other rumours insisted that after the beheading, Cromwell's torso was not buried beneath the gallows but had been retrieved from the stables of a nearby tavern by Cromwell's grieving daughter Mary, second wife of Thomas Belasyse, first Earl Fauconberg, a Councillor of State, and Ambassador at Venice and Paris. In order to save her father's remains from further desecration, it was alleged that she took them home with her to Newburgh Priory near Coxwold in North Yorkshire. There the remains have been variously reported as being entombed in what became known as 'Cromwell's Room', an enclosed space at the top of a large and elaborate porch, or in a small bricked-off compartment, about four feet high, beneath a sloping roof of rough planks in the attic. Since then the tomb, wherever situated, has remained unopened despite many pleas to the contrary, by personages as celebrated as King Edward VII who, when Prince of Wales, was a guest staying in the house. Even were the mausoleum to be opened, it would be extremely difficult to identify its contents as being the remains of Cromwell, as the absence of a head would probably be an almost insurmountable complication, although DNA tests with those of descendants might provide more acceptable proof.

On 5 February, six days after the hideous charade on the scaffold, Samuel Pepys witnessed the heads of Cromwell and his erstwhile colleagues 'set up upon the further end of the Westminster Hall'. There it remained for over forty years, eventually being dislodged during the great storm of 1703. It was found by a sentry sheltering from the gale who, according to reports in the *Daily Chronicle* of 1895 and the *Daily Mail* of 1904, concealed it under his cloak, took it home, and hid it in his chimney. On his deathbed he divulged the fact to his wife, and it is said that she sold it to one Herr du Puy, a museum owner (a gentleman once mentioned in *Pepys Diary*), for in 1710 a German visitor to London, Zacharias Conrad von Uffenbach, saw the head, described by its then owner as 'one of his greatest curiosities, that could easily be sold for as much as sixty guineas'. At that von Uffenbach commented 'I was surprised that these English could still have such affection and respect for this monstrous head; for there are still many such heads to be found in England, many of them too quite ready for such an elevated position'.

The head was next reported in 1773 as being in the possession of Samuel Russell, one of the Cambridge branch of Cromwell's family through his daughter Mary. Reportedly he offered it to Cromwell's old college, Sidney Sussex but, the offer being declined, Samuel, described as 'a poor comedian' decided to augment his meagre income by exhibiting his relative's head for a fee in Covent Garden. This innovative idea proved to be quite a lucrative business, the visiting public even included personages as illustrious as the famous painter Joshua Reynolds who viewed the head in 1786.

In 1787 it was picked up 'as a bargain for £118' by one James Cox or Fox, variously described as an antiquarian dealer or a showman. This gentleman also exhibited the macabre specimen, employing as 'curator' one John Cranch, who later publicised it via the media, the advertisement in the *Morning Chronicle* of 18 March 1799 proclaiming; 'The Real Embalmed Head of the Powerful and Renowned Usurper Oliver Cromwell is now exhibited at 5 Mead Court, Old Bond Street, where the rattlesnake was shown last year; a genuine narrative relating to its Acquisition, Concealment and Preservation is to be had at the Place of Exhibition. Tickets Half a Crown'.

In 1812 Cox, or Fox, parted with the exhibit to three nieces of the last surviving member of the family for £230; they, understandably nervous at possessing such a gruesome heirloom, persuaded their medical adviser, Dr. Josiah Wilkinson, to buy it from them (although it is not known why they simply didn't give the relic a decent burial). The good doctor accordingly acquired it, preserved in the identical silk-lined box in which it had been placed by the Russells.

As the head had been embalmed, it was still in a fair state of preservation; the famous wart on the forehead was visible, while the nose was flattened to the right side of the face. Among those privileged to view the relic was John Flaxman, a notable sculptor, who, on being asked by what characteristics would he identify it, replied 'I know a lot about its configuration and there is one feature which will be a crucial test; instead of having the lower jawbone somewhat curved, it was particularly short and straight, but set out at an angle which gave him a jowlish appearance'. The relic was duly examined, and answered exactly to the sculptor's description, the length from the forehead to the back of the head being stated as quite extraordinary. Some time later Doctor Wilkinson's assistant reported that he had noticed this unusual physiological feature in a patient of theirs, and subsequent enquiries revealed that the man's name was Williams, the Cromwell family name, and he claimed descent from him.

By 1865 it was in the possession of another of the Wilkinson family, Mr W A Wilkinson of Beckenham, Kent and, despite the manhandling undergone by the head over the centuries, the spike on which it had been impaled for display on Westminster Hall, entering underneath the lower jaw and piercing the skull, was still in situ, John Timbs FSA describing how 'in the part above the crown of the head, (the pike) is worn almost as thin as a bodkin by having been subjected to the variations of the weather, but the part within the skull which is protected by its situation, is not so much corroded. The woodwork (the shaft of the pike), part of which remains, is so much worm-eaten that it cannot be touched without crumbling'.

From time to time endeavours had been made to institute an official inquiry to ascertain the authenticity of the skull, but in 1911 Mr Asquith, the Prime Minister, refused to set one up. However in March of that year the head, then owned by the Rev Horace R Wilkinson of Woodbridge, Suffolk, was exhibited at the Royal Archaeological Institute, and that worthy clergyman gave a lecture on the subject. Public figures, among them Sir Henry Howarth and Dr Boyd Dawkins, both eminent antiquaries, declared the skull to be indubitably that of Cromwell. Twenty years later, in 1932, the head was loaned by the Wilkinsons to the Faculty of Medicine of the London University, where Professor Karl Pearson and Dr G M Morant among others were producing a book illustrating every known picture of Cromwell. Following a wide ranging analysis of records, measurements, X-ray pictures, portraits and sculptures of the subject, together with a comparison with a copy of his death mask earlier owned by Sir Richard Tangye, the professor and his colleagues, although admitting that at first they had started the enquiry in a sceptical frame of mind, nevertheless had reached the conclusion that the head was that of a man aged about sixty who had been decapitated after death, who would have worn a hat of six and seven-eighths inches in size, whose brain cavity was 1500 cubic centimetres, whose skull had earlier been trepanned for embalming purposes, and whose other physical characteristics, even to the impression of a wart above the eye socket, was indeed that of Oliver Cromwell. The expert opinion of the renowned Master of the Tower Armouries, Charles ffoulkes, was sought, to determine the authenticity or otherwise of the spike involved. He confirmed that because of its design it was indeed a seventeenth century fighting weapon, and after a further examination revealed that a worm-hole had penetrated both the broken shaft and the skull, he had little doubt that both head and pike had been aligned in that position for over two centuries. Accordingly, in 1935, the book entitled *Portraiture of Oliver Cromwell, with Special Reference to the Wilkinson Head* was duly published confirming its authenticity.

Five years or so later the head was subjected to a medical examination by a highly skilled surgeon, Mr Dickson Wright. He wrote: 'The first thing I looked for was the historical wart which Cromwell insisted on his portrait painters putting in, and there in the proper place was the depression from which it had been chipped. Then I looked for the little beard that one sees in all his pictures, and it was there, as was his moustache. The long curly head of hair was gone, but it was easy to see that Cromwell was not bald when he died, but had a complete head of reddish hair. Then I looked for the marks of the axe on the back of his neck, and the marks of six blows of the axe were plainly to be seen. Now there is in existence an eye-witness's account of the execution which says it took eight blows of the axe to sever the head because of the embalming cloths wrapped around the neck. The teeth are almost gone, and the lips broken. The nose is flattened and pushed to one side; one would expect this to occur while the head was being chopped off'.

The relic subsequently passed to Canon Horace Wilkinson of Woodbridge, Suffolk (one assumes a relative of the Rev Wilkinson previously mentioned?) by whom, in 1960, it was again bequeathed to Cromwell's old college, Sidney Sussex, in Cambridge and this time accepted. There, on an oval plaque at the left hand side of the chapel entrance, is inscribed the words:

> 'Near to this place was buried on 25 March 1960 the head of OLIVER CROMWELL Lord Protector of the Commonwealth of England, Scotland and Ireland. Fellow Commoner of this College 1616-17'.

A fitting end to a grim saga.

Some body parts were of course removed with honourable intent. Following Napoleon's death, his heart was removed and buried separately from his body, in a silver container of spirits. Many years later, both were exhumed and taken to Paris, where they were ceremonially re-interred.

In many cases, heads of those executed were claimed and, instead of being decently interred by grieving relatives, were kept by them, a practice based on the not unnatural belief that the head, containing the brain, the very 'being' and so the soul of the person, actually was the loved one, the body being the impersonal 'back-up' system to keep the 'head' nourished and alive. So when St. Thomas More was executed by the axe and his head piked on London Bridge as a deterrent to all who might have the temerity to disagree with Henry VIII, his daughter Meg Roper managed to claim it from the Bridge's watchman and kept it with her until she died, her son then cherishing it until his death, when it was buried in the Roper tomb in the Church of St Magnus the Martyr in Canterbury. It was later reported that the lower jawbone had been stolen, resulting in an iron grille being secured across the niche in which it was housed. The Saint's body is of course buried in the crypt of the Royal Chapel of St Peter ad Vincula within the Tower of London.

Another head retained by its family was that of Sir Walter Raleigh, Lady Raleigh placing it in a velvet-lined bag after his decapitation by the public executioner. At her death it remained with their son Carew, with whom it was eventually buried in the family church in Surrey.

If it is true, a fascinating story surrounds the heart of James Graham, Marquis of Montrose. After his death his heart was removed and placed in a gold box which in turn was housed in a metal case made from the blade of his sword. It went missing, later coming into the possession of a descendant, John Napier. It was said that the heart was subsequently taken to India by another member of the family, who was wounded during a fracas with the French but the heart survived and, viewed as a talisman, was bought by an Indian rajah who, on learning of the Marquis' exploits and prowess, returned it to the family. Regretfully, however, it was lost during the time of the French Revolution, and was never recovered.

There are obviously no limits to the depths to which people descend in their judgment of what constitutes a souvenir, even the skeleton of a murderess being classed as worthwhile. When twenty-one year old Jane Scott murdered her mother in 1828 by administering rat poison to her and was sentenced to death at Lancaster, she became so emaciated during her imprisonment that she was wheeled to the scaffold in a child's high-chair. On the drop the noose was placed round her neck, the chair withdrawn, and Jane paid the price of her crime. But there was no burial, Christian or otherwise for her, her corpse being purchased by a Dr Thomas Monk who practised in the neighbouring town of Preston. When he died some sixty years later, the wired-up skeleton was acquired by a herbalist, Mr Livesy. After some initial repugnance, 'Old Jane' as she was nicknamed, became one of the family, her yellowing appearance being improved by the application of a coat of whitewash, though this was somewhat marred by a pink spot on her skull where rain had dripped on her from a leaky roof. The Livesy grandchildren accepted her as an unprotesting and highly flexible playmate, occasionally using her forearms as drumsticks. However during a burglary at the herbal shop, the skull was stolen, and when the family eventually moved away, some of the bones were buried in the garden, and others presented to a local museum.

As one researches ancient records on this particular subject, one begins to wonder just how many occupants of coffins still in fact retain their heads! A report circulated some years ago, emanating from a man named Roger Quinn, known in the Borders as the 'Tramp Poet', to the effect that when he was a boy, he was playing in a churchyard in Dumfries when a man beckoned to him. On Roger approaching him, the stranger placed a skull in his hands and said, 'Now, laddie, you will be able to tell people all your life that you once held the skull of Robbie Burns in your hands'. The man may have been one of the officials charged with exhuming the poet's corpse and transferring it to a mausoleum which had been specially erected in Burns' honour. It was also alleged that when the grave was opened up for the burial of the poet's wife, someone stole the skull in order to take a cast of it.

Another poet whose remains were separated was Percy Bysshe Shelley who died in 1822. His corpse was cremated but when it was discovered that his heart remained unconsumed by the flames, it was placed in a vase, preserved in spirits and while his ashes were interred in the Protestant cemetery in Rome, his heart was buried in Bournemouth.

Still on the subject of poets, much controversy has raged over the identity of a corpse vandalised in 1790 in St Giles Church, Cripplegate. The remains were believed by many to be those of John Milton who died on 8 November 1674 and when it was proposed to erect a suitable monument in his memory, the coffin was inspected by Messrs Thomas Strong, solicitor, and John Cole, Churchwarden. An account of what happened was published in *A Narrative of the Disinterment of Milton's Bones in the Parish Church of St Giles, Cripplegate* which described how by the help of a candle they proceeded to where the coffin lay. It was in chalky soil and in digging through the whole space where the ground was opened, they failed to find any other coffin which could raise the slightest doubt of this being Milton's. Despite cleaning its surface, no inscription, initials or date could be found but, satisfied by its position in the chancel that it was indeed Milton's, the ground was closed again.

Immediately following his investigations Mr Cole had a somewhat convivial evening with friends and, the conversation turning to the day's events, his acquaintances Laming and Fountain expressed a desire to see the remains. Mr Cole agreed, provided that the grave had not yet been filled in again. The next morning the party met at the church and between them they pulled the coffin to the edge of the grave by means of a corroded hole in the leaden lid. Another companion, Holmes, then obtained a mallet and chisel and proceeded to hack open both the ends of the lid. Bending the lead back, the body was immediately visible, swathed in the folds of its shroud; upon disturbing the fabric, the ribs collapsed but, undeterred by this,

Mr Fountain leant over and pulled hard at the teeth, which resisted until someone hit them a knock with a stone, when they easily came out. There were only five in the upper jaw, all sound and white, and Mr Fountain, having forcibly extracted all of them, generously gave one to Mr Laming, the latter gentleman also 'liberating' one from the lower jaw, followed by Mr Taylor who took two. Mr Laming was heard to say that he had a good mind to take the whole lower jaw; he had it in his hand, but then tossed it back again.

Worse was to follow, for Laming and Taylor went home to get some scissors with which to cut off the hair; however, this was found unnecessary, persuasion with a stick easily removing it, and when the men had obtained all the souvenirs they required and had left, a female grave-digger, Elizabeth, took over. With an eye to increasing her doubtless meagre income, she decided to put the corpse on public display – at a price of course. As the coffin was situated under one of the pews, she kept a tinder-box nearby and when interested members of the public entered, she struck a light and conducted them to the cavity where, pulling the lid back, she exhibited the cadaver, at first for sixpence, later dropping the price to threepence, then twopence per person. Other employees got in on the act, the workmen in the church refusing to unlock the doors until a pot of beer had been handed over, though to avoid paying many got in at the window at the west end of the church.

The *Narrative* then concluded its account by reporting 'that Ellis, a comedian (!) who was skilled in dressing hair, took a lot of it from the corpse, together with a rib bone wrapped in paper, under his coat. Hawkesworth, a journeyman, took a tooth and a bit of the ribs and later sold them. And after being open for the greater part of two days, the grave was eventually filled in'. Doubt was expressed from many quarters about the true identity of the corpse, but there was no doubt at all over the indignities inflicted upon it.

After World War II, one of the female concentration camp guards, Irma Grese, was found guilty of using the skin of dead prisoners-of-war to make lamp-shades. She was hanged, and it is to be regretted that a similar use was not made of hers, for this practice was quite widespread even as early as the sixteenth century. An edict issued by the Barber-Surgeons states that; 'no p'son or p'sons of the Companie do presume at any tyme or tymes hereafter of Anathomies to take and carry awaie or cause to be taken or carried awaie ant p'te of the skynn of anie bodie whiche shall at anie tyme hereafter happen to be wrought upon within the hall of the mysterie and the same tann or cause to be tanned like lether upon the payne of Vli' (a fine of 7s).

In more recent centuries the hides of hanged felons were distributed – at a price – as souvenirs, a notable case occurring in March 1809 when Mary Bateman was hanged at York. She had left her job as housemaid to set up in business as a fortune-teller in Leeds, combining her art with extorting money and property from her clients as the price of prophesying their future. Her greed driving her to commit murder, the 'Yorkshire Witch' as she became known, was sentenced to be hanged. Thousands of spectators jostled round the scaffold, many breathlessly waiting for her to exercise her supernatural powers and vanish into thin air the moment the noose tightened around her neck. But when it did, she didn't!

Back in Leeds, twenty-three miles away, a crowd of nearly two and a half thousand people, having paid threepence each to see the body on its return, waited patiently until, at midnight, the hearse finally arrived and the viewing commenced. The proceeds from the morbid exhibition totalled £30 and this swelled the coffers of the Leeds General Infirmary, where the corpse was later dissected. (One wonders whether such a practice, if re-introduced, could solve some of the financial problems of the NHS.) In accordance with tradition, her skin was peeled off and tanned, then distributed in small pieces to those who applied and, as reported in the *Folklore of Yorkshire* published in 1901, parts of her skin were on sale in Ilkley as late as 1892. Doubtless the witch's remains were advertised in the appropriately named magazine.

APPENDIX I

PAMPHLET:THE USE OF THE DEAD TO THE LIVING.

Southwood Smith's *Pamphlet*, containing his well-reasoned, albeit long-winded, arguments in favour of dissection, even at the cost of taking no action against body snatchers, was distributed among Members of Parliament and, together with other factors, was responsible for the passing of the *Anatomy Act* of 1832, which legalised the use of corpses for dissection subject to various conditions. Although minor extracts from it have been included in the previous chapters, further relevant excerpts are included here.

The Pamphlet is preceded by an *Advertisement*, i.e. *Introduction*, as follows;

The substance of the following pages, which first appeared in the *Westminster Review*, was reprinted in the form of a Pamphlet in the year 1824, the intention being to send a copy of it to every Member of Parliament. But, in deference to what was understood to be the wish of the administration at that time, the discussion of the question was postponed, and the distribution of the pamphlet was therefore delayed. The subject is now before the consideration of the Legislature. An attempt is made in these pages to show, by reference to facts, which the unprofessional reader can understand, why it is that dissection is indispensable; to point out the true nature and extent of the obstacles which at present oppose this pursuit, and to state the measures which appear likely to afford easy and effectual relief. Every Member of the Legislature, into whose hands this pamphlet may fall, is most respectfully but earnestly intreated calmly and candidly to consider the facts adduced, to show the absolute necessity of providing in some mode for the prosecution of this pursuit. What that mode is, there can now be no doubt. The legislative interference required is extremely simple. All that is necessary is, first to repeal that part of the existing law which imposes dissection as a punishment; and secondly, to enact, that the bodies of persons who die in hospitals and in work-houses, unclaimed by immediate relatives, be appropriated to the purpose of dissection.

Were the later measure adopted, it is certain that the different parishes in London alone would afford a most ample supply. If the reader will take the trouble to cast his eye over the following pages, he will probably be satisfied that there has seldom occurred a case in which it was possible to accomplish so great a public good, by means at once so easy and so effectual.

USE OF THE DEAD TO THE LIVING

Every one desires to live as long as he can. Everyone values health 'above all gold and treasure.' Every one knows that, as far as his own individual good is concerned, protracted life and a frame of body sound and strong, free from the thousand pains which flesh is heir to, are unspeakably more important than all other objects, because life and health must be secured before any possible result of any possible circumstance can be of consequence to him. In improvement of the art which has for its object the preservation of health and life, every individual is, therefore, deeply interested. An enlightened physician and a skilful surgeon, are in the daily habit of administering to their fellow men more real and unquestionable good, than is communicated, or communicable by any other class of human beings to another. Ignorant physicians and surgeons are the most deadly enemies of the community; the plague itself is not so destructive; its ravages are at distant intervals, and are accompanied with open and alarming notice of its purpose and power; theirs are constant, silent, secretive; and it is while they are looked up to as saviours, with the confidence of hope, that they give speed to the progress of disease, and certainty to the stroke of death.

It is deeply to be lamented that the community, in general, are so entirely ignorant of all that relates to the art and science of medicine. An explanation of the functions of the animal economy; of their most common and important deviations from a healthy state; of the remedies best adapted to restore them to a sound condition, and of the mode in which they operate, so far as that is known, ought to form a part of every course of liberal education. The profound ignorance of the people on all these subjects is attended with many disadvantages to themselves, and operates unfavourably on the medical character. In consequent of this want of information, persons neither know what are the attainments of the man in whose hands they place their life, nor what they ought to be; they can neither form an opinion of the course of education which it is incumbent upon him to follow, nor judge of the success with which he has availed himself of the means of knowledge which have been afforded him.

There is one branch of medical education in particular, the foundation. in fact, on which the whole superstructure must be raised, the necessity of which is not commonly understood, but which requires only to be stated to be perceived. Perhaps it is impossible to name any one subject which is of more importance that the community should understand. It is one in which every man's ignorance or information will have some influence. We shall, therefore, show the kind of knowledge that the physician and the surgeon should possess; we shall illustrate, by a reference to particular cases, the reason why knowledge of this kind cannot be dispensed with; and we shall explain, by a statement of facts, the nature and extent of the obstacles which at present oppose the acquisition of this knowledge. We repeat, there is no subject in which every reader can be so immediately and deeply interested, and we trust that he will give us his calm and unprejudiced attention.

The basis of all medical and surgical knowledge is anatomy. Not a single step can be made either in medicine or surgery, considered either as an art or a science, without it. This should seem self-evident, and to need neither proof nor illustration; nevertheless as it is useful occasionally to contemplate the evidence of important truth, we shall show why it is that there can be no rational medicine, and no safe surgery, without a thorough knowledge of anatomy.

Disease, which is the object of these arts to prevent and to cure, is denoted by disordered function; disordered function cannot be understood without a knowledge of healthy function; healthy function cannot be understood without a knowledge of structure; structure cannot be understood unless it be examined.

The organs on which all the important functions of the human body depend, are concealed from the view. There is no possibility of ascertaining their situation and connections, much less their nature and operation, without inspecting the interior of this curious and complicated machine. The results of the mechanism are visible; the mechanism itself is concealed, and must be investigated to be perceived. The operations of nature are seldom entirely hidden from the human eye; still less are they obtruded upon it, but over the most curious and wonderful operations of the animal economy so thick a veil is drawn, that they could never have been perceived without the most patient and minute research. The circulation of the blood, for example, could never have been discovered without dissection. Notwithstanding the partial knowledge of anatomy which must have been acquired by the accidents to the human body is exposed, by attention to wounded men, by the observance of bodies killed by violence; by the huntsman in using his prey; by the priest of immolating his victims; by the augur in pursuing his divinations; by the slaughter of animals, by the dissections of brutes; and even occasionally by the dissection of the human body.

In the 14th century, Mundinus, professor at Bologna, astonished the world by the public dissection of two human bodies. In the 15th century, Leonardo da Vinci contributed essentially to the progress of the art by the introduction of anatomical plates which were admirably executed. In the 16th century the Emperor Charles V ordered a consultation to be held by the divines of Salamanca to determine whether it was lawful, in point of conscience, to dissect a dead body in order to learn its structure. In the 17th century Cortesius, professor of anatomy at Bologna, and afterwards professor of medicine at Messina, had long begun a treaty on practical anatomy which he had an earnest to finish, but so great was the difficulty of presenting the study even in Italy, that in 24 years he could only twice procure an opportunity of dissecting a human body, and even then with difficulty and in a hurry; whereas he had expected to have done so, he says, once every year, according to the custom of the famous academies of Italy. In Muscovy, until very lately, both anatomy and the use of skeletons was positively forbidden, the first as inhuman, and the latter as subservient to witchcraft. Even the illustrious Luther was so biased by the prejudices of his age that he ascribed the majority of diseases to the arts of the devil, and found great fault with physicians when they attempted to account for them by natural causes. England acquired the bad fame of being the country of witches, and opposed almost insuperable obstacles to the cultivation of anatomy.

Even at present (1828 - author) the prejudices of the people on this subject are violent and deeply-rooted. The measure of that violence may be estimated by the degree of abhorrence with which they regard those persons who are employed to procure the subjects necessary for dissection. In this country there is no other method of obtaining subjects but that of exhumation; aversion to this employment may be pardoned; dislike to the persons who engage in it is natural, but to regard them with detestation, to exult in their punishment, to determine for themselves its nature and measure, and to endeavour to assume the power of inflicting it with their own hands, is absurd. Magistrates have too often fostered the prejudices of the people and afforded them the means of execution, their vengeance on the objects of their aversion.

The press, with a few honourable exceptions, has uniformly allied itself with the ignorance and violence of the vulgar, and has done everything in its power to inflame the passions which it was its duty to endeavour to soothe. It is notorious that the winter before last there was scarcely a week in which many of the papers did not contain the most exaggerated and disgusting statements; the appetite which could be gratified with such representations was sufficiently degraded, but still more base was the servility which could pander to it.

As one among many of the cases which illustrate this bad feeling, we may refer to that of Samuel Clark who was indicted at the Essex Quarter Sessions in January 1824 for feloniously stealing at Little Leighs on the 26 of December, a woman's shift, a bed-gown, a night-cap and a pair of cotton stockings, the property of James Chinnery. It appeared in evidence that a young woman, the wife of a labouring man named James Chinnery, had been buried in Little Leighs Church-yard on Sunday the 21st of December. Previous to her death she expressed a wish to be interred in a night-cap, shift, bed-gown and cotton stockings, and her request had been complied with.

The body was discovered in the morning of the 26th, in a ditch near the Church-yard. A few rods from this spot was found a horse yoked to a chaise cart and tied to a tree. It appeared that 'the box under the chaise cart was calculated to hold a couple of human bodies, when rolled up; and on examining it, a most offensive odour proceeded from it, as if it had recently been used in the prisoner's 'unhallowed' occupation.' The prisoner owned this horse and cart, and this is the whole of the evidence, at least, as stated in the report of the trial, which implicated him in the robbery of the grave. Under these circumstances the counsel for the prisoner submitted to the Court that there was no case to go to the jury, on three grounds;- first, that there was no proof of any asportation (theft, removing without permission) of the articles alleged to have been stolen; secondly that supposing the asportavit made out, the prisoner could not be convicted of this offence unless it was manifest that he had a felonious intention of taking the clothes and converting them to his own use; and thirdly, that in all events, there was no evidence upon which the jury could safely be called up to act, so as to implicate him in the alleged offence.

The council for the prosecution in answer urged, first, that the finding of the body, naked, after proof that it had been interred in the clothes mentioned in the evidence, was sufficient proof of asportation; and that even stripping the body without removing the clothes out of the grave was, in law, enough to support the indictment; secondly, that although the primary intention of the prisoner might be, to steal the body only, yet, if the clothes were taken, the law would construe them to have been feloniously taken; that it might as well be said that although a man's intention might be to steal a valuable jewel, yet it was no offence to take the casket in which it was contained; and thirdly, that whether the defendant was the party to whom guilt was imputed, was a question solely for the consideration of the jury.

On the prisoner's counsel insisting that his objections had not been answered, the Chairman overruled the first two objections and then summed up the evidence, on which the jury, after deliberating a few minutes, found the prisoner 'Guilty'. The verdict, it is recorded, 'was received by the auditory (audience, those in the public gallery) with a general expression of pleasure.' The Court, after animadverting in strong terms on the 'abominable' offence of which the prisoner had been found guilty, said they were determined that he should not have an opportunity of pursuing his 'odious' trade in this country for at least some years, and therefore sentenced him to be transported for seven years.

The account of this case is taken from the report of the trial contained in the *Globe and Traveller* newspaper of Jan. 20, 1824, a paper honourably distinguished for its endeavours to enlighten the public mind on this subject, not to foster its prejudices. In this case there was no sufficient evidence to convict the prisoner of the alleged offence; even if that evidence had been perfectly satisfactory, the punishment inflicted was unjust; the circumstance essential to constitute the felony did not exist; the Chairman, with an ignorant and vulgar mind, stretched the law to gratify an ignorant and vulgar prejudice; he relied upon the public feeling for protection in the illegal exertion of his power; he administered the law badly; he endeavoured to justify his conduct by loading the prisoner with odious epithets, and he did not miscalculate the feeling of his auditory; they witnessed the transaction 'with a general feeling of pleasure'. This case exhibits but too faithfully, the spirit often displayed both by the magistracy and the people.

Half a century ago there was in Scotland no difficulty in obtaining the subjects which were necessary to supply the schools of anatomy. The consequence was, that medicine and surgery suddenly assumed new life - started from the torpor in which they had been spell- bound - and made an immediate and rapid, and brilliant progress. The new seminaries constantly sent into the world men of the most splendid abilities, at once demonstrating the excellence of the schools in which they were educated, and rendering them illustrious. Pupils flocked to them from all quarters of the globe and they essentially contributed to that advancement of science which the present age has witnessed. In the 19th century the good people of Scotland, that intelligent, that cool and calculating, that most reasonable and thinking people, have thought proper to return to the worst feeling and the worst conduct of the darkest periods of antiquity.

There is at present no offence whatever which seems to have such power to heat and to exalt into a kind of torrent the blood which usually flows so calmly and sluggishly in the veins of a Scotchman. The people of 1823 - to compare great things with small - emulate the spirit of those of their forefathers who were 'out in the forty-five'; the object, to be sure, is somewhat different, but it is amusing to see the intensity and seriousness of the excitement. About twelve months ago an honest farmer of the name of Scott, who resides at Linlithgow, apprehended a poor wight who was pursuing his vocation, we presume, in the church-yard of that place, and this service appeared so meritorious to the people in his neighbourhood that they presented Scott with a piece of plate.

In the winter sessions of 1822/3 a body was discovered on its way to the lecture room of an anatomist in Glasgow, and in spite of the exertions of the police, aided by those of the military, this gentleman's premises and their contents, which were valuable, were entirely destroyed by the mob. For some time after this achievement, it was necessary to station a military guard at the houses of all the medical professors in that city. In the spring of the justiciary court last year at Stirling, while the judges were proceeding to the court, the procession was assaulted with missiles; several persons were injured and it was necessary to call in the protection of a military force. The object of the mob was to inflict summary punishment of a man who was about to be tried for the exhumation of a body.

We happen to know that the most disgraceful proceedings were some time ago instituted in that town against a young man of respectable family and connections, who was in fact expatriated and whose prospects in life were entirely changed, if not ruined, because he had too much honour to implicate his instructors in a transaction which would have put them to inconvenience, and in which they had engaged from a desire faithfully to discharge their duties to their pupils (I understand this means that the surgeons, his instructors, needing a body for instructional purposes, engaged him to procure a corpse but he was caught and deported - another case, the conviction in which was deemed by Smith as being against the law -author). Within the last five years three men were lodged in the county gaol at Haddington, charged with trespass in the church-yard of that town. So enraged were the mob against them, that an attempt was made to force the gaol in order to get at them. On their way to the court, the men were again attacked, forced from the carriage and severely maimed. After examination they were admitted to bail but, when set to liberty, they were assailed with more violence than ever, and were nearly killed.

A similar assault was some time ago made on two American

gentlemen who went to visit the Abbey of Linlithgow after nightfall. The church-yard of the 'gude Scots' are now strictly guarded by men and dogs; watch towers are now erected within the grounds, and 'mort-safes' as they are called, that is to say, strong iron frames, are deposited in the ground over the graves. These people sometimes declare that they will put an end to anatomy, and certainly they are succeeding in the accomplishment of this menace as rapidly as they can well desire.

The average number of medical students in Edinburgh is 700 each session. For several years the difficulty of procuring subjects (bodies as specimens) in that place has been so great that out of all that number, not more than 150 or 200 have ever attempted to dissect, and even these have latterly been so opposed in their endeavours to prosecute their studies that many of them have left the place in disgust. We have been informed by a friend that he alone was personally acquainted with twenty individuals who retired from it at the beginning of last session, and who went to pursue their studies at Dublin, and we know that vast numbers followed their example at the end of the winter course. The medical school at Edinburgh, in fact, is now subsisting entirely on its past reputation; in the course of a few years it will certainly be at an end, unless the system is changed. Let those who have the prosperity of the University at heart, and have the power to protect it, consider this before it be too late; they may be assured it is no idle prediction, for we give them notice that it is at this moment the universal opinion and the current language of every well-informed medical man in England.

An excellent system of anatomical plates, which has been well-received by the profession, has lately been published by Mr Lizars, a lecturer on anatomy and physiology, in Edinburgh. This gentleman states that he has been induced to undertake the work in order to obviate the most fatal consequences to the public; as far, at least, as a reference to art, instead of nature, is capable of obviating these consequences. He affirms that the difficulty of obtaining instruction from nature (i.e. the real thing - dead bodies) has risen to such a pitch, owing to the extraordinary severity exercised by the legal authorities of the kingdom against persons employed in procuring subjects for dissection, as to threaten the ultimate destruction of medical and anatomical science. In his preface to the second part of his work he apologizes to his readers for dividing one portion from another, with which it ought to have been connected, but states that he has been compelled to, from the prejudices of the place, which prevented him for upwards of five months from procuring a subject from which he might make his drawings. 'In place of living' he says 'in a civilized and enlightened period, we appear as if we had been thrown back some centuries into the dark ages of ignorance, bigotry and superstition. Prejudices, worthy only of the multitude, have been conjured up and appealed to, in order to call forth popular indignation against those whose business it is to exhibit demonstratively the structure of the human body and the function of its different organs. The public journals, from a vicious propensity to pander to the vulgar appetite for excitement, have raked up an industriously circulated stories of the exhumation of dead bodies, tending to exasperate and inflame the passions of the mob; and persons who, by their own showing, are friendly to the interests of science have, in the excess of their zeal that bodies should remain undisturbed in their progress to decomposition, laboured to destroy in this country, that art, whose province it is, to free living bodies from the consequences inseparable for accident and disease. And which is worst of all, the prejudices of the multitude have been confirmed and rendered inveterate by the proceedings in our courts of justice, which have visited (sentenced) with the punishment due only to felons, the unhappy persons necessarily employed in the present state of the law, in procuring subjects for the dissecting room.'

He then goes on to state that, until anatomy be publicly sanctioned in Edinburgh, the school of medicine there can never flourish; that upon the present system, young men obtain a degree or a diploma after a year or two of grinding, that is, of learning by rote the answers to the questions which the examiners are in the habit of putting to the candidates; that ignorant of the very elements of their profession, numbers of persons thus educated annually go to the East and West Indies and to the army and navy, where they have charge of hundreds of their suffering fellow creatures, to whom they are, in fact, the instruments of cruelty and murder.

In the preface to the 4th. Part, he adds, that when Part II was published, in the early part of the session, he took occasion to express his sorrow for the degraded state of his profession, and the threatened ruin of the Medical School of his native place, owing to the scarcity of subjects (specimens); that, for doing this, he has incurred considerable censure; that he regrets that he has found no reason to alter his opinion, for the winter session is now near its conclusion and he candidly declares that such had been the scarcity of material, that 'no teacher of anatomy or surgery has been able either to follow the regular plan of his course, or to do his duty to his pupils'; the consequence of which has been, that many of the students have left the school in disgust and gone either to Dublin or Paris; while a still greater number, deprived of the means of dissecting, have contented themselves with lectures, theories, and with grinding; and entered on the practice of their profession ignorant of its fundamental principles.

Much of this opposition on the part of the people arises from the present mode of procuring subjects. Fortunately there is, in Great Britain, no custom, no superstition, no law and, we may add, no prejudice against anatomy itself. There is even a general conviction of its necessity; there may be a feeling that it is a repulsive employment, but it is commonly acknowledged that it must not be neglected. The opposition which is made, is made, not against anatomy, but against the practice of exhumation; and it is this practice which ought to be opposed. It is, in the highest degree, revolting; it would be disgraceful to a horde of savages; every feeling of the human heart rises up against it; so long as no other means of procuring bodies for dissection are provided, it must be tolerated, but in itself it is alike odious to the ignorant and the enlightened, to the most uncultivated and the most refined.

But the capital objection to this practice is, that it necessarily creates a crime and educates a race of criminals. Exhumation is forbidden by the law. It is indeed prohibited by no statute, either in England or in Scotland; in both it is an offence punishable by common law. There is a statute of James the First, which makes it a felony to steal a dead body for the purpose of witchcraft; there is none against the taking of a body for dissection. In the case of the King against Lynn in 1788 the Court decided that the body being taken for the latter purpose did not make it a less indictable offence; and that it is without doubt cognizable in a criminal court because it is an act 'highly indecent; at the bare idea of which nature revolts.' It is punishable therefore, by fine or imprisonment or both; in Scotland it is also punishable by whipping and even by transportation.

We expected better things of America. We cannot express our astonishment and indignation when we found that the State of New York had actually made it a felony to remove a body from the place of sepulchre for the purpose of dissection, without providing in any other mode for the schools of anatomy. This is worse than any thing that exists in any other part of the world. If these pages should reach the eyes of any of our American friends, we intreat them to read with attention, the facts which have been stated in the former part of this pamphlet and consider the mischief they are doing. It will not be believed in England that such scenes can have been witnessed in America, as were actually exhibited there scarcely a month ago (then followed the episode quoted in an earlier chapter regarding the keeper of the Potter's Field sending his dog in to arrest a body snatcher, who was subsequently sentenced to six months in the Penitentiary - author). The judge declared "The gentlemen attending the Medical School of this city will take warning by this man's fate. They may rest assured that the keeper of Potter's field will do his duty, and public justice will be executed on any man, whatever may be his condition in life, who is found violating the law, and the decency of Christian burial!" We do not blame the Americans for abolishing the practice of exhumation, but we blame them for stopping there. We maintain that it is both absurd and criminal to make this practice felony without providing in some other method for the cultivation of anatomy.

In Great Britain the law against the practice of exhumation is not allowed to slumber. There may be other cases which have not come to our knowledge, but we have ascertained that there have been 114 convictions for England alone during the past year. The punishments inflicted have been imprisonment for various periods, with fines of different sums. The fines in general are heavy, considering the poverty of the offenders. Several persons are, at this moment, suffering these penalties; among others, there is now in the gaol of St Albans, a man who was sentenced for this offence to two years imprisonment and a fine of £20. The period of his confinement has expired some time, but he still remains in prison on account of his inability to pay the fine. Since the passing of the new *Vagrant Act*, it has been the common practice to commit these offenders to hard labour for various periods. Very lately, two men, convicted of this offence, were sent to the Tread-Mill in Cold Bath Fields gaol, one of whom died in one month after his conviction.

It is an error to suppose that these punishments operate to prevent exhumation; their only effect is to raise the price of subjects; a little reflection will show that they can have no other operation. At present exhumation is the only method by which subjects can be procured; but subjects for this purpose MUST be procured, and, be the difficulties what they may, WILL be procured; diseases will occur, operations must be performed, medical men must be educated, anatomy must be studied, dissections must go on. Unless some other means for affording a supply be adopted; whatever be the law or the popular feeling, neither magistrates, nor judges, nor juries, will, or can put an entire stop to the practice. It is one which, from the absolute necessity of the case, must be allowed. What is the consequence? So long as the practice of exhumation continues, a race of men must be trained to violate the law. These men must go out in company for the purpose of nightly plunder, and plunder of the most odious kind, tending in a peculiar and most alarming measure to brutify the mind and to eradicate every feeling and sentiment worthy of a man. This employment becomes a school in which men are trained for the commission of the most daring and inhuman crimes. Its operation is similar, but much worse than the nightly banding to violate the game laws, because there is something in the violation of the grave which tends still more to degrade the character and to harden the heart. This offence is connived at, nay, rewarded; these men are absolutely paid to violate the law, and paid by men of reputation and influence on society. The transition is but too easy to the commission of other offences in the hope of similar connivance, if not similar reward.

It is an odious thing that the teachers of anatomy should be brought into contact with such men; that they should be obliged to employ them, and that they should even be in their power; which they are to such a degree that they are obliged to bear with the wantonness of their tyranny and insult. All the clamour against these men only operate to raise the premium on the repetition of their offence. This premium the teachers of anatomy are obliged to pay, which these men perfectly understand, who do not at all dislike the opposition which is made to their vocation. It gives them no unreasonable pretext for exorbitancy in their demands. In general they are men of infamous character; some of them are thieves, others are the companions and abettors of thieves. Almost all of them are extremely destitute. When apprehended for the offence in question, the teachers of anatomy are obliged to pay the expenses of the trial and to support their families while they are in prison; whence this idea of immunity is associated, in these men's minds, with the violation of the law, and when they do happen to incur its penalties, they practically find that they and their families are provided for, and this provision comes to them in the shape of a reward for the commission of their offence. The operation of such an system on the minds of the individuals themselves is extremely pernicious, and is not a little dangerous to the community.

Moreover by the method of exhumation, the supply after all is scanty; it is never adequate to the needs of the schools; it is of necessity precarious, and it sometimes fails altogether for several months. But it is of the utmost importance that it should be abundant, regular, and cheap. The number of young men who come to London for the purpose of studying anatomy and surgery may be about a thousand. Their expenses are necessarily very considerable while they are in town; they have already paid a large sum for their apprenticeship in the country; the circumstances of country practitioners, in general, can but ill-afford protracted expenses for their sons in London; few of them stay a month longer than the time prescribed by the College of Surgeons. But the short period they spend in London is the only time they have for acquiring the knowledge of their profession. If they mis-spend these precious hours, or if the means of employing them properly be denied them, they must necessarily remain ignorant of life. After they leave London they have no means of dissection. We have seen that it is by dissecting alone, that they can make themselves acquainted even with the principles of their art; that without it they cannot so much avail themselves of the opportunities of improvement, which experience itself may offer, nor, without the highest temerity, perform a single operation. We have seen that occasions suddenly occur, which require the prompt performance of important and difficult operations; we have seen that, unless such operations are performed immediately, and with the utmost skill, life is inevitably lost. In many such cases there is no time to send for other assistance. If a country practitioner - and most of these young men go to the country - be not himself capable of doing what is proper to be done, the death of the patient is certain. We put it to the reader to imagine what the feelings of an ingenuous young man must be, who is aware of what he ought to do, but who is conscious that his knowledge is not sufficient to authorise him to attempt to perform it, and who sees his patient die before him, when he knows he might be saved and that it would have been in his own power to save him, had he been properly educated. We put it to the reader to conceive what his own sensations would be, were an ignorant surgeon, with a rashness more fatal than the criminal modesty of the former, to undertake an important operation. Suppose it were a tumour, which turned to be an aneurysm; suppose it were a hernia, in operating on which the epigastric artery were divided, of the intestine itself wounded; suppose it were his mother, his wife, his sister, his child, whom he thus saw perish before his eyes, what would the reader then think of the prejudice which withholds from the surgeon that information without which the practice of his profession is murder?

The study of anatomy is a severe and laborious study; the practice of dissection is on many accounts highly repulsive; it is even not without danger to life itself - a winter never passes without proving fatal to several students who die from injuries received in dissection. To men of clear understandings, to those especially of a philosophical turn of mind, the pursuit is its own reward; they are so fully satisfied that the more it is cultivated the more satisfaction it will afford, that they need no stimulus to induce them to undergo the drudgery. But this is by no means the case with ordinary minds. The fatigue and disgust of the dissecting rooms are appalling to them, and they need the stimulus of necessity to urge them to the task. The court of examiners of the College of Surgeons requires from the candidate for surgical diplomas, certificates that they have gone through at least two courses of dissections; the examiners at Apothecaries-hall do not require such certificates. The consequence is, that many young men content themselves with attending lectures and with passing examinations at Apothecaries-hall, and do not apply for a diplöma at the College of Surgeons, This single fact is sufficient to demonstrate to the public that, instead of throwing obstacles in the way of dissection, it is a duty which they owe to themselves to afford every possible facility to its practice, and to hold out to every member of the profession, the most powerful inducements to engage in it, by rewarding with confidence those who cultivate anatomy, by making excellence in anatomy indispensable to all offices in dispensaries and hospitals, and by thus rendering it impossible for anyone who is ignorant of anatomy, to obtain rank in his profession.

When a candidate presents himself for a diploma in Denmark, in his first trial he is put into a room with a subject (corpse), a case of instruments, and a memorandum, and informed that he is to display the anatomy of the face and neck, or that of the upper extremity, or that of the lower extremity; that by the anatomy, is to be understood the blood-vessels, nerves and muscles; and that as soon as he has accomplished his task, his professors will attend his summons, to judge of his attainments. These professors are the true examiners!

We shall have entered into the discussion of this subject to little purpose if we have not produced in the minds of our readers a deep conviction that anatomy ought to form an essential part of medical education; that anatomy cannot be studied without the practice of dissection; that dissection cannot be practiced without a supply of subjects, and that the manner in which the supply is obtained in England is detestable and ought immediately to be changed.

The plan we would propose to substitute is the following;

1. That the bodies of those persons who die in all infirmaries and hospitals throughout the kingdom, *unclaimed by immediate relatives* (Smith's italics), be appropriated to the purpose of anatomy.

2. That the bodies of those persons who die in all work-houses and poor-houses be appropriated to the same purpose.

3. That the bodies of those persons who die in all houses of corrections, in all prisons and in the hulks (prison-ships moored permanently in harbour), be thus appropriated.

Any objection may be anticipated to such an appropriation of the bodies of those who die in infirmaries and hospitals. And it is admitted that in the present state of public feeling, it would not be right thus to appropriate the bodies of ALL who die in those public charities. But this is not proposed; what is proposed is to appropriate to this use the bodies of those ONLY who die unclaimed by immediate relatives. No reasonable objection can be urged to this measure thus guarded. No one who has not inquired into the subject can have any conception of the number of persons who die in the public hospitals in London, unvisited by friends during life, unclaimed by them after death. Surely to devote to this use the bodies of those who die under such circumstances can inflict no wound on any private individual - can violate no public right. Still there is one objection to the measure which is specious but not solid. It is urged that it might be the means of deterring this class of persons from entering the hospitals. The answer to this objection is complete, because it is the answer derived from experience. The measure has been actually adopted, and found in practice to be unattended with this result; it was tried in Edinburgh and the hospital was as full as it is at present; it is universally acted on in France, and the hospitals are always crowded.

It was adopted in Edinburgh with perfect success more than a century ago. In the *Council Register* for 1694, it is recorded that all unclaimed bodies in the charitable institutions or in the streets, were given for dissection to the College of Surgeons, to one or two of its individual members, and to the professor of anatomy. This regulation, at that period, excited no opposition on the part of the people, but effectually answered the desired object. All the medical schools on the continent are supplied with subjects, by public authority, in a similar manner.

The following account of the mode in which those of Paris in particular are supplied, has been obtained from the gentleman who is at the head of the anatomical department in the city. It is stated;

1. That the faculty of medicine at Paris is authorized to take from the civil hospitals, from the prisons, and from depots of mendacity, the bodies which are necessary for teaching anatomy.

2. That a gratuity of eight-pence is given to the attendants in the hospitals for each body.

3. That upon the foundation by the National Convention, of schools and health, the statutes of their foundation declare, that the subjects necessary for the schools of anatomy shall be taken from the hospitals, and that since this period, the

council of hospitals and the prefect of police have always permitted the practice.

4. That M. Breschet, chief of the anatomical department of the faculty of Paris, sends a carriage daily to the different hospitals, which brings back the necessary number of bodies; that this number has sometimes amounted to 2000 per annum, for the faculty only, without reckoning those used in L'Hôpital de la Pitié but that since the general attention which has recently been bestowed upon pathologic anatomy, numbers of bodies are opened in the civil and military hospitals, and that the faculty seldom obtain more than 1000 or 1200.

5. That, beside the dissections by the faculty of medicine, and those purchased in L'Hôpital de la Pitié, theatres of anatomy are opened in all the great hospitals for the pupils of those establishments; that in these institutions anatomy is carefully taught, and that pupils have all the facilities that can be desired.

6. That the price of a body varies from four shillings to eight shillings and sixpence.

7. That after dissection, the bodies are wrapped in cloth and carried to the neighbouring cemeteries, where they are received for tenpence.

8. That the practice of exhumation is abolished; that there are insurmountable obstacles to the return to that system, and that bodies are never taken from burial grounds without an order for exhumation, which is given only when the tribunal require it for the purpose of medico-legal investigations.

9. That though the people have an aversion to the operations of dissection, yet they never make any opposition to them, provided respect be paid to the laws of decency and salubrity, on account of the deep conviction that prevails of their utility.

10. That the relatives of the deceased seldom or never oppose the opening of any body, if the physicians desire it. That all the medical students in France, with scarcely any

exception, dissect, and that that physician or surgeon who is not acquainted with anatomy is universally regarded as the most ignorant of men.

To the other parts of the plan proposed above for supplying the anatomical schools in Great Britain, there appears to be no objections whatsoever. No one can object to such a disposal of the bodies of those who die in poor-houses. These persons are pensioners upon the public bounty; they owe the public a debt; they have been supported by the public during life; if, therefore, after death they can be made useful to the public. It is a prejudice, not a reason - it is an act of injustice, not the observance of a duty, which would prevent them from becoming so. It is true that many of these persons are honest and respectable, and may have been reduced to indigence by misfortune; were they all so, it would not alter the state of the argument. Some concession and co-operation on the part of the public, for this great public object, is indispensable, without which nothing can be done; but if any concession be made, it can be made with respect to this class of person better than any other, because it can be made with less violation of public feeling. Neither is any indignity either intended or offered to these persons. They are appropriated to this service not because they are poor, but because they are friendless; because, that is, no persons survive them who take such an interest in their fate as to be rendered unhappy by this disposal of their remains. That they are without friends is no good reason why their memory should be treated with indignity; but it is a good reason, it is the best possible reason why they should be selected for this public service. Poverty, it is true, is a misfortune, has pain and terror enough in itself; no legislature ought by any act to increase its wretchedness; but the measure here proposed is pregnant with good to the poor, and would tend more than can be estimated to lessen the misery of their condition. For it would give knowledge to the lowest practitioners of the medical art, that is, to the persons who are at present lamentably deficient, and into whose hands the great bulk of the poor fall. And after all, the true question is, whether the surgeon shall be allowed to gain knowledge by operating on the bodies of the dead, or driven to obtain it by practising on the bodies of the living. If the dead bodies of the poor are not appropriated to this use, their living bodies must be - and will be.

The rich will always have it in their power to select, for the performance of an operation, the surgeon who has signalized himself by success; but that surgeon, if he have not obtained the dexterity which ensures success by dissecting and operating on the dead, must have acquired it by making experiments on the living bodies of the poor. There are no other means by which he can possibly have gained the necessary information. Every such surgeon who has attained deserved eminence, must have risen to it through the suffering which he has inflicted, and the dead which he has brought upon hundreds of the poor. What would be the immediate and constant effect of an abolition of the practice of dissecting the dead? It would be to convert poor-houses and public hospitals into so many schools where the surgeons, by practising on the living bodies of the poor, would learn to operate on those of the rich with safety and dexterity. Thus the poor would be tortured and many of them would be put to death in order that the rich might be saved from pain and danger. This would be the inevitable result - this would indeed be to treat this class of the people with real indignity and horrible injustice, and proves how possible it is to show an apparent consideration for the poor, and yet practically to abuse them in the most cruel manner.

The plan now proposed for remedying the evils which have been stated, would accomplish the object easily and completely; it would inflict no injury on any private individual; it would inflict no violence to the public feeling; it would render the dread of anatomy, as far as that dread were really operative, directly beneficial to the community; it would terminate at once the evils of the present system; it would put an end to the education of daring and desperate violators of the law; it would tranquillize the public mind; the dead would rest undisturbed; the sepulchre would be sacred, and all the horrors which the imagination connects with its violation would cease forever.

We submit these observations to the calm and serious consideration of our countrymen. We address them especially to the members of our legislature. Upon the attention of the latter we would particularly urge this matter further consideration, the importance of which they well know how to estimate. In consequence of the difficulty of procuring subjects in England, every student in Great Britain who can possibly afford the time now goes to Paris to perfect himself in anatomy. Accordingly the number of English students in Paris is already immense; that number increases rapidly every year; it increases by the desertion of the schools in Edinburgh and London. The consequence is obvious, and will surely and deeply be felt in a few years.

Anatomy will be neglected in England and for this indispensable branch of knowledge, England will become entirely dependent on France. There cannot be a doubt that there is good sense enough among the people of England to submit to whatever regulations may be necessary to prevent evils so serious and so fatal, provided such regulations are framed in a proper spirit, and observed with a due regard for decorum, and it is certain that those persons who co-operate to establish these regulations will ultimately receive, as they will deserve, the gratitude of their country.

SELECT BIBLIOGRAPHY

Annals of the Barber-Surgeons of London, S Young, London 1890

Being an Account of Tomb Despoilers, S Ogden, Brendon & Nonsough, 1894

Catalogue, Museum of Anatomy, Liverpool, 1877

Celebrated Trials of All Countries, Philadelphia, 1835

Curiosities of Town and Countryside, E Vale, 1940

Dead Men Tell Tales, Richard Haestier, John Long Ltd, 1938

Diary of a Resurrectionist, J B Bailey, Sonnenschein, 1896

Devils, Drugs and Doctors, H W Haggard, Heinemann, 1929

Doings in London, Smeaton, 1828

Edinburgh, M G Williamson, Methuen, 1906

History of Burke and Hare, G MacGregor, Morison, 1884

The Inhumanists, C H Turner, 1932

International Criminals Past and Present, F Boutet, 1934

Life of Sir Robert Christison, Edinburgh, 1885

Life of Sir Astley Cooper, B B Cooper, 1843

Life of Charles Darwin and his Published Letters, F Darwin, 1892

Life of John Hunter, J Foot, 1794

The Life of Sir Richard Owen, R Owen, London 1894

London Rediscoveries, W G Bell, 1929

London Stories, John o' London, 1926

Newgate Calendar, Werner Laurie, 1933

North Country Lore and Legend, Walter Scott, 1888

Notes and Queries of Galloway, 1910

Pageant of London, R Davey, 1906

Romance of London, J Timbs, 1865

The Sack 'em Up Men, J M Ball, 1928

Sixty Famous Trials, P Hoskins, 1936

Some Account of London, T Pennant, 1793

Strange Pages from Family Papers, T F Dyer, Sampson, Low, 1895

Tyburn Gallows, London County Council, 1909

Tyburn Tree, A Marks, Brown, Langham, 1908

Use of the Dead to the Living, S Smith, Baldwin & Cradock, 1828

INDEX